MORE ALABAMA

DAILY DEVOTIONS FOR DIE-HARD FANS

CRIMSON TIDE

MORE ALABAMA

Also Available
Daily Devotions for Die-Hard Fans: Alabama Crimson Tide
and
Daily Devotions for Die-Hard Kids: Alabama Crimson Tide

More Daily Devotions for Die-Hard Fans: Alabama Crimson Tide
© 2015, 2017 Ed McMinn
Extra Point Publishers; P.O. Box 871; Perry GA 31069

Unless otherwise noted, scripture quotations are taken from the *Holy
Bible, New International Version.* Copyright © 1973, 1978, 1984, by the
International Bible Society. Used by permission of Zondervan.

Cover design by John Powell and Slynn McMinn
Interior design by Slynn McMinn

Visit us at die-hardfans.com.

CRIMSON TIDE

Daily Devotions for Die-Hard Fans
Available Titles

ACC
Clemson Tigers
Duke Blue Devils
FSU Seminoles
Georgia Tech Yellow Jackets
North Carolina Tar Heels
NC State Wolfpack
Notre Dame Fighting Irish
Virginia Cavaliers
Virginia Tech Hokies

BIG 10
Michigan Wolverines
Michigan State Spartans
Nebraska Cornhuskers
Ohio State Buckeyes
Penn State Nittany Lions

BIG 12
Baylor Bears
Oklahoma Sooners
Oklahoma State Cowboys
TCU Horned Frogs
Texas Longhorns
Texas Tech Red Raiders
West Virginia Mountaineers

SEC
Alabama Crimson Tide
MORE Alabama Crimson Tide
Arkansas Razorbacks
Auburn Tigers
MORE Auburn Tigers
Florida Gators
Georgia Bulldogs
MORE Georgia Bulldogs
Kentucky Wildcats
LSU Tigers
Mississippi State Bulldogs
Missouri Tigers
Ole Miss Rebels
South Carolina Gamecocks
MORE South Carolina Gamecocks
Texas A&M Aggies
Tennessee Volunteers

and *NASCAR*

Daily Devotions for Die-Hard Kids
Available Titles
Alabama, Auburn, Baylor, Georgia, LSU
Miss. State, Ole Miss, Texas, Texas A&M

---

die-hardfans.com

MORE ALABAMA

DAILY DEVOTIONS FOR DIE-HARD FANS

CRIMSON TIDE

DAY 1

GO FOR IT

Read Matthew 4:18-22.

"[A]nd immediately they left the boat and their father and followed him" (v. 22).

Some of his friends told Chris Donnelly he was making the biggest mistake of his young life. Still, he took a chance.

Donnelly was the SEC's Freshman of the Year in 1989 as a safety at Vanderbilt. His sophomore year the reality of playing on a team apparently destined to lose set in. The Commodores were 2-20 his two seasons in Nashville. "I reached a point where I stopped believing," he said. When his head coach was fired after the 1990 season, he requested and received his release to transfer.

Donnelly's list of destinations was a short one: Alabama. Right away, "he was hit with a wave of skepticism." "I had friends . . . who wanted to know why I would give up a $60,000 a year Vanderbilt education to ride the bench at Alabama," he recalled. "They all said, 'You'll never play there.'"

Transfer rules required him to sit out a season. On the scout team, he learned the Alabama defensive system under coordinator Bill "Brother" Oliver. The time on the bench and his track record as a proven SEC performer served him well. When the 1992 season started, so did Donnelly, at safety.

And this wasn't just any defense. One writer said the Alabama defense of 1992 "has been the gold standard for UA defenses ever since." In 2012, another writer said that defense is still "considered the best modern day unit in SEC history." The team won the national title, and the defense gave up only 55 yards per game rushing and only 9.4 points per game. Donnelly had 52 tackles, three interceptions, and six pass breakups.

He started also in '93 as a senior. The chance Chris Donnelly took turned out to be a good deal for him and for Alabama.

As it was with Chris Donnelly, our lives are the sum total of the chances we have taken — or have not taken — along the way. Every decision we make every day involves taking a chance. Maybe it will work out for the better; maybe it won't. We won't know unless we take a chance.

On the other hand, our regrets often center on the chances we pass by. The missed chance that has the most destructive and devastating effect on our lives comes when we fail to follow Jesus. He calls us all to surrender to him, to commit to him exactly as he called Simon, Andrew, James, and John.

What they did is unsettling. Without hesitation, without telling Jesus to give them time to think about it or wrap up the loose ends of their lives or tell all their friends good-bye, they walked away from a productive living and from their families. They took a chance on this itinerant preacher.

So must we. What have we got to lose? Nothing worthwhile. What have we got to gain? Everlasting life with God. If that's not worth taking a chance on, nothing is.

Transferring to Alabama made me who I am.
> — *Chris Donnelly on the chance he took*

To take a chance and surrender our lives to Jesus is to trade hopelessness and death for hope and life.

DAY 2

HAVE A GOOD DAY

Read Psalm 34.

"Whoever of you loves life and desires to see many good days, keep your tongue from evil and your lips from speaking lies" (vv. 12-13).

To say that A.J. McCarron had a good day in the 2012 Iron Bowl is a vast understatement. His day crossed over into the blessed.

Alabama was on the way to its fifteenth national title; Auburn was 3-8. So much for any real suspense surrounding the game of Nov. 24. Led by its junior quarterback, the Alabama offense quickly and methodically crushed what little hope the Auburn faithful had of ruining the Tide's season. The first-team offense scored a touchdown on each of its first seven possessions. The 49-0 smashing was the most one-sided game in the series since Alabama won 55-0 in 1948.

Freshman wide receiver Amari Cooper grabbed five passes for 109 yards and two touchdowns. Junior running back Eddie Lacy contributed 131 yards and two touchdowns on 18 carries.

The day, however, belonged to McCarron who "was as good as anyone could ask him to be." He completed 15 of 21 passes for 216 yards and four touchdowns and was "faultless in his decision-making."

That last part is where McCarron really excelled, changing plays at the line of scrimmage in response to the way Auburn's defense lined up. Such excellence wasn't just luck and skill. Mc-

Carron spent the week studying Auburn until during the game "he was able to read the Tigers' defense like a children's book."

When Auburn had two safeties deep, McCarron checked to a run. With one safety back, he went to a pass. "The result, in chess terms, was checkmate." McCarron also spent the day spotting holes in the Auburn defense and faultlessly checking from one run or pass play to another to take advantage of the weakness.

A.J. McCarron had a day that was blessed, and the Tide rolled.

It's commonplace today. Someone performs a service for you — a counter clerk, a waiter, a porter — and their parting shot is a cheerful, "Have a good day!" It's the world's wish for us as if it is the culmination of everything the world has to offer.

For those who put their faith and their trust in the world, it is. They can't hope for anything better because they turn to an inadequate source.

There is something much better, however, than a mere "good" day. It's a "blessed" day. It's a day that, as the psalmist envisions it, is much more than simply managing to make it through twenty-four hours without a catastrophe or heartbreak. It's a day in which God manifests his goodness by pouring out blessings upon us.

How do we transform a routine "good" day into an awesome "blessed" day? We trust and obey almighty God rather than the machinations and the people of this world. For God, having a good day simply isn't good enough. For us, it shouldn't be either.

I felt like I knew what they were going to do every play.
— *A.J. McCarron on his 2012 game against Auburn*

The world offers a good day;
God offers a blessed day.

DAY 3

REDEEMED

Read 1 Peter 1:17-25.

"It was not with perishable things such as silver or gold that you were redeemed from the empty way of life handed down to you from your forefathers, but with the precious blood of Christ" (vv. 18-19).

When Justin Thomas learned Alabama's men's golf team had redeemed itself, he took off running in the opposite direction his shot had just taken.

In 2012, the Tide golfers suffered a bitterly disappointing 3-2 loss to Texas in the finals of the NCAA men's golf championship. That loss was never far from the team's collective mind as the 2013 season unfolded. Senior captain Scott Strohmeyer and Thomas, who was the national player of the year in 2012 as a freshman, watched replays of the national-championship loss repeatedly.

Seeking some sweet redemption, the team made it back to the championship tournament in 2013, and there they were in the finals on Sunday, June 2, against Illinois. A few hours before play began, coach Jay Seawell gathered his team together to deliver a simple message: "Let's go get it." The coach admitted he normally would never say such a thing at a team meeting, but he had seen the fire in his players' eyes. "We wanted this," he said. "This was our chance, our opportunity" at redemption.

And the golfers seized their chance. They crushed Illinois 4-1 for the school's first-ever title. Bobby Wyatt, Trey Mullinax, Strohmeyer, and Cory Whitsett all won their matches.

The only Illinois point came when Thomas simply stopped playing and conceded so he could celebrate the team's title and its redemption with his teammates. He had just hit his approach shot on No. 18 when he received the news from a tournament official that the Tide's win was official. He took off running and didn't stop until he got to the 15th green where the national champions were gathered.

In our capitalistic society, we know all about redemption. Just think "rebate" or store or product coupons. To receive the rebates or the discount, though, we must redeem them, cash them in.

"Redemption" is a business term; it reconciles a debt, restoring one party to favor by making amends as was the case with Alabama's 2013 golf team in gaining the title it had lost in 2012. In the Bible, a slave could obtain his freedom only upon the paying of money by a redeemer. In other words, redemption involves the cancelling of a debt the individual cannot pay on his own.

While literal, physical slavery is incomprehensible to us today, we nevertheless live much like slaves in our relationship to sin. On our own, we cannot escape from its consequence, which is death. We need a redeemer, someone to pay the debt that gives us the forgiveness from sin we cannot give ourselves.

We have such a redeemer. He is Jesus Christ, who paid our debt not with money, but with his own blood.

Not too many teams get to be here two years in a row.
  — Justin Thomas on Alabama's chance at NCAA redemption

**To accept Jesus Christ as your savior is to believe
that his death was a selfless act of redemption.**

DAY 4

WHAT A SURPRISE!

Read 1 Thessalonians 5:1-11.

"But you, brothers, are not in darkness so that this day should surprise you like a thief" (v. 4).

C.J. Mosley was totally surprised when teammates voted him the Most Valuable Player of the 2012 team. His surprise was really not surprising since he was only a part-time starter.

Mosley was not even listed as a starting linebacker for the BCS national championship game against Notre Dame on Jan. 7, 2013. That wasn't surprising either since he was officially credited with only eight starts during the regular season. Still, he led the team with 107 tackles and was a first-team All-America. He made what was dubbed the most important play of Alabama's national championship season. He tipped a last-second pass in the SEC championship game, a play that preserved the 32-28 win over Georgia and propelled Alabama into the BCS title game.

Mosley was a star (who went on to a pro career after another All-American season as a senior). That he wasn't a full-time starter was a testament to the success of the rotating defense employed by Nick Saban and his defensive coordinator, Kirby Smart. When Alabama was in its "normal" defense against the rush, the inside linebackers were Nico Johnson and Trey DePriest.

Fortunately for Mosley and the Tide, Alabama used its base defense only about 20 percent of the time in 2012. That put Mosley on the field for most of the plays even though he may not have been officially listed as the starter.

At the team banquet, Mosley was stunned when his name was called as the team's MVP. At the time, his mouth was full of cake. "When I heard it, I had to eat [the cake] up real quick to get out there," he said about the surprise announcement.

Some surprises in life — such as C.J. Mosley's MVP award — provide us with experiences that are both joyful and delightful. Surprise birthday parties are a delight. And what's the fun of opening Christmas presents when we already know what's in them?

Generally, though, we expend energy and resources to avoid most surprises and the impact they may have upon our lives. We may be surprised by the exact timing of a baby's arrival, but we nevertheless have the bags packed beforehand and the nursery all set for its occupant. Paul used this very image (v. 3) to describe the Day of the Lord, when Jesus will return to claim his own and establish his kingdom. We may be caught by surprise, but we must still be ready.

The consequences of being caught unprepared by a baby's insistence on being born are serious indeed. They pale, however, beside the eternal effects of not being ready when Jesus returns. We prepare ourselves just as Paul told us to (v. 8): We live in faith, hope, and love, ever on the alert for that great, promised day.

They asked me to say something, but I was shocked and didn't want to go up there and start mumbling.
— C.J. Mosley on being named the team's MVP

The timing of Jesus' return will be a surprise;
the consequences should not be.

DAY 5

THE OPPORTUNITY

Read Colossians 4:2-6.

"[M]ake the most of every opportunity" (v. 5b).

Colenzo Hubbard got an opportunity he never saw coming: to play football for the University of Alabama.

"It was still during the time of segregation," The Rev. Hubbard recalled years later. "I never thought I'd have a chance to go to school at Alabama." When he visited the campus in 1971 with a friend who was being recruited, "It was like Disneyland. I never dreamed it was possible for me to go there."

But it was. Bear Bryant and his staff liked what they saw in Hubbard. On an official visit in 1972, they told him he could play for Alabama if he made his grades. "I went home and began studying from the time I got off the bus from school until after midnight," Hubbard said. He graduated with honors.

He was a part-time starter at noseguard from 1973 to 1976. Every day he still wears his 1973 national championship ring.

His greatest moment came in the Mississippi State game of 1976, which he didn't start. The Bulldogs led 17-0 at halftime. Normally soft-spoken, Hubbard stunned everybody by interrupting the Bear to ask if he could say something. "I must have had a brief moment of insanity," Hubbard said. Bryant let him talk.

"I'm a senior and we're down," he said. "But if it depends on me whether or not we'll win the game, the guy I'll play against will not beat me. We can win this game."

Five minutes into the second half, Bryant bellowed, "Where's Colenzo Hubbard?" He jogged onto the field thinking, "I've got to prove what I said." He did. He had ten tackles, a fumble recovery, two interceptions, and a sack. The Tide won 34-17.

Hubbard made the most of his opportunity. Ken Donahue, his position coach, told him, "You accomplished more in the limited time you played than any player I've ever coached."

Opportunities usually give us only one shot at them. Miss the chance and it's gone forever. The house you wanted that came on the market; that chance for promotion that opened up, the accidental meeting with that person you've been attracted to at a distance: If the opportunity comes, you have to grab it right now or you may well miss it.

This doesn't hold true in our faith life, however. Salvation through Jesus Christ is not a one-and-done deal. As long as we live, every day and every minute of our life, the opportunity to turn to Jesus is always with us. We have unlimited access to the saving grace of our Lord and Savior.

As with any opportunity, though, we must avail ourselves of it. That is, salvation is ours for the taking but we must take it. The inherent tragedy of an unsaved life thus is not that the opportunity for salvation was withdrawn or unavailable, but that it was squandered.

Alabama gave me an opportunity, and the work I do every day repays the opportunity given to me.
— The Rev. Colenzo Hubbard, who works with impoverished children

We have the opportunity for salvation through Jesus Christ at any time.

DAY 6

ROCK BOTTOM

Read Psalm 23.

"Even though I walk through the valley of the shadow of death, I will fear no evil for you are with me; your rod and your staff, they comfort me" (v. 4).

Jeremy Shelley hit rock bottom on Nov. 5, 2011, in the 9-6 loss to LSU. He then climbed to the mountaintop on Jan. 9, 2012, in the 21-0 defeat of LSU.

Alabama's kicking game was an unmitigated disaster in the regular-season showdown against the top-ranked Tigers. In a game described as "one of the titanic struggles of the college football season," the Tide attempted six field goals and made only two. One try was blocked.

Cade Foster, the long-range kicker, abandoned his Facebook page after the game because of the unrelenting criticism. Shelley, however, accepted the vitriol in stride. "I still got some hate mail here and there," he admitted, "but I also had a lot of people behind me."

Then came the unprecedented rematch in January for the BCS national championship. Naturally, the first Alabama scoring chance was with a field goal. Shelley nailed it. He admitted that the kick was "nerve-racking," considering the earlier LSU game. "Once I hit that first one, I was like, 'All right, let's keep this going.'"

He had a moment, though, of *deja vu*. LSU's block of his second attempt "unleashed a torrent of Groundhog Day jokes in the press box. . . . On Twitter . . . everyone hunkered down for a carbon copy of the first game."

Not on this night. Shelley scored all the points in the first half. His three field goals gave Alabama a 9-0 lead. When the game ended, Bama had a 21-0 shellacking of the Tigers and a national title, and Shelley had tied a bowl record with five field goals.

"Shelley, you're my hero," declared junior defensive end Jesse Williams as he passed Shelley in the locker room after the game. "I love you."

Jeremy Shelley had kicked his way out of rock bottom.

Maybe it was the day your business went under, taking everything you owned with it. Or the night your spouse walked out. Or the afternoon you learned your child was seriously, perhaps deathly, ill. You've known rock bottom.

Rock bottom is the time when life is its darkest. You are down in a dark valley looking up the mountain peaks where the sun shines and people laugh and have hope. Rock bottom is the time when life is its loneliest, when "friends" and acquaintances desert you and the train wreck that is your life.

And yet in that darkness and that loneliness, you will find your best friend. You will find Jesus, who's been in that valley ahead of you. He knows sorrow, suffering, loss, and pain. Trust in him and he'll take you where he wound up after he walked through that valley; he'll take you all the way to glory.

Lowest of lows, highest of highs.
— *Jeremy Shelley on the difference in the two LSU games*

**'Nobody knows what I'm going through!';
Jesus does because he's been there.**

STEAL THE SHOW

Read Luke 10:30-37.

"'Which of these three do you think was a neighbor to the man who fell into the hands of robbers?'" (v. 36)

Ben Eblen didn't score very much, but he sure could come up with a steal at the right time.

A reserve point guard from 2009-12, Eblen's role on the court was clearly defined. "Definitely on the defensive end," he once said about where he was called on to excel. "Not necessarily shoot the ball but get everybody in the offense."

Eblen took quite seriously that part about not shooting the ball very much. One writer encouraged fans to watch Eblen's play: "He will come open for an outside shot, and he will pause. Then he will dribble or pass."

Eblen shot so rarely that as a junior in 2011-12, he scored only nine points in 29 games. His sophomore season he also averaged less than one point per game.

That indifference toward scoring didn't affect his value to the team. "I have a chance to play every night, "Eblen said, "just because Coach [Anthony] Grant hones on defense."

That defense was never more evident than when the 12th-ranked Kentucky Wildcats swaggered into Tuscaloosa on Jan. 18, 2011. The Tide was on its way to a 25-win season that included a 12-4 record in the SEC and a runner-up spot in the NIT.

For much of the game, Bama played like the better team, taking a 52-32 lead five minutes into the second half. But the Cats rallied and closed to within 67-66 in the closing seconds. Kentucky had the ball with a chance to hit the game-winning shot.

Clutch defensive specialist that he was, Eblen made the game-saving play, a steal at the perimeter. Kentucky fouled him with 2.8 seconds left, and he hit one free throw, his only point of the game. The Cats could manage only a hopeless half-court shot.

Alabama had stolen a 68-66 win.

Rare is the person of faith who can't quote God's eighth commandment: You shall not steal. That's pretty direct, but implicit in that order is a divine recognition of the right to personal property. Something can't be stolen if it isn't owned.

Theft in America is pandemic. From the penny-ante shoplifters to those who pad their expense accounts to the wealthy who lie and cheat on their taxes to the swindlers with a pyramid scheme. The prevalent attitude — like the robbers in Jesus' parable of the Good Samaritan — is that I will take your stuff because I can.

That doesn't make it right, especially in God's eyes. In fact, the attitude toward possessions that the person of faith should have is exemplified by the Good Samaritan himself: What is mine is yours to share if you have need of it.

The truth is that what we call "our" money and "our" stuff is really God's. To use it in ways other than those God has ordained is nothing less than stealing from God. As a result, we may ultimately rob ourselves of our eternal salvation.

We're driving to the wing and [Ben Eblen] muscles [my guy] off.
— UK head coach John Calipari explaining Eblen's game-saving steal

'You shall not steal.' God meant it.

STEAL THE SHOW   15

DAY 8

POWER PLAY

Read Psalm 147:1-18.

"Great is our Lord and mighty in power" (v. 5a).

In case anyone entertains any doubt about Bear Bryant being the real power in college football during his day, check out how the pairing for the 1976 Sugar Bowl was arranged.

Top-ranked Alabama's 24-3 demolition of 18th-ranked Penn State on Sept. 11, 2010, marked the first time the two teams had played in twenty years. The matchup also sparked memories of the Bear's games against Joe Paterno.

Paterno never beat Bryant; he was 0-4. The Nittany Lions coach once wrote that the legendary 1979 Sugar Bowl, which the Tide won 14-7 to win the national title, hurt the worst. That '79 classic was the second time the two coaching legends had met in the Sugar Bowl. They squared off in what was technically the 1976 Sugar Bowl, which was played on New Year's Eve. It was the first college football game played in the New Orleans Superdome. The pairing wasn't an accident; Bryant arranged it.

Jay Paterno, the coach's son and an assistant coach, recalled that Bryant called his father and said he wanted to invite him to the Sugar Bowl. Not surprisingly, the head coach asked the Bear if he were authorized to extend the invitation. Paterno didn't want to take his team off the bowl market on the basis of a promise that turned out to be empty. "Don't worry about it," Bryant said. "If I say I'm going to play you in the Sugar Bowl, I'm going to play you." Paterno contacted the Sugar Bowl boss, who confirmed that if Bryant wanted to play him, the teams would play.

Joe Paterno had one more question for Bryant: Why Penn State since other available teams would be ranked higher? Bryant's answer was blunt and earthy: "Because you're not that good and we're going to kick your [backside]."

The power broker got the game he wanted and a 13-6 win.

No power of any man or woman — not even Bear Bryant — can come close to matching that of almighty God. After all, he's not called "almighty" for nothing.

As Psalm 147 tells us, God determined how many stars to hang and knows the name of each one. He heals the brokenhearted, paints the sky with his clouds, and controls the weather. His understanding is without limits. In short, God is the lord of all creation, including rocks, bugs, and the air itself.

Yet, God's power has his limits. Some are intrinsic and some are self-imposed, but they are real. God cannot do everything.

For instance, he cannot lie. He cannot break a promise, including that one about never wiping us out with another flood. God cannot change, nor can he sin. He cannot be wrong; he cannot die. Especially intriguing is that God cannot learn anything new.

One more: God can never stop loving us. Thus, he can never rescind his offer of salvation through his son Jesus Christ, no matter how many times we exert our own power and refuse it.

No bowl made a move in the 1970s until [Bear] Bryant decided what Alabama would do.
— Writer Ivan Maisel on the power the Bear wielded

God's power has limits; his love for us doesn't.

THE BIG TIME

Read Revelation 21:22-27; 22:1-6.

"They will see his face, and his name will be on their foreheads. . . . And they will reign for ever and ever" (vv. 22:4, 5c).

Nick Saban's mandate was clear: Return Alabama football to the big time. For the Tide, that meant being the best.

In the spring of 2007, 92,000 Alabama fans showed up for the spring game, a glorified scrimmage. They were there to see Saban as much as they were there to see the team.

Back in January, "done with waiting, with mediocrity and with disappointment," the Alabama powers-that-be had lured Saban away from the Miami Dolphins. They "paid him enough money to burn a wet dog," writer Rick Bragg said, and the faithful "welcomed him as Caesar, as pharaoh."

Why Nick Saban? "We wanted a man who had won a championship," explained athletic director Mal Moore. Even if that national title had been won at division rival LSU of all places.

At Alabama, the past is always present. The larger-than-life figures of Wallace Wade and Bear Bryant and the expectations they left behind still loom large. But Wade's last season in Tuscaloosa was 1930; Bryant retired following the 1982 season. With the exception of Gene Stallings, who won a national title in 1992, "The comparison with Bryant has smothered the coaches who've come after him," Bragg wrote. After Stallings "came everything but locusts." Thus, the call to Saban went out.

So how have Alabama's Caesar and his players handled the pressure at "the most storied, demanding and impatient program in college football?" Very nicely. Through the 2016 season, Saban's teams had won 119 games and lost only 19. Most importantly, they were national champions in 2009, 2011, 2012, and 2015.

The Tide has assumed its rightful position in college football's hierarchy as the biggest big-time program of them all.

Like the Alabama football program did in 2007, we often look around at our current situation and dream of hitting the big time. We might look longingly at that vice-president's office or daydream about the day when we're the boss, maybe even of our own business. We may scheme about ways to make a lot of money, or at least more than we're making now. We may even consciously seek out fame and power.

Making it big is just part of the American dream. It's the heart of that which drives immigrants to leave everything they know and come to this country.

But all of this so-called "big-time" stuff we so earnestly cherish is actually only small potatoes. If we want to speak of what is the real big-time, we better think about God and his dwelling place in Heaven. There we not only see God and Jesus face to face, but we reign. God puts us in charge. Now *that's* the big time.

There is never anything wrong with remembering the past, but you can't live in it.
— *Mal Moore after his hire of Nick Saban*

**Living with God, hanging out with Jesus,
reigning in Heaven — now that's big time.**

DAY 10

A FAST START

Read Acts 2:40-47.

"Everyone was filled with awe. . . . [They] ate together with glad and sincere hearts, praising God and enjoying the favor of all the people" (vv. 43a, 46b, 47a).

A recurring theme of Alabama's preparation for the national championship game against Notre Dame was the need to get off to a fast start. Probably no one, not even the players themselves, envisioned just how fast their start would be.

The Fighting Irish were ranked No. 1 heading into the BCS National Championship Game of Jan. 7, 2013. That ranking seems ludicrous in light of the way the game turned out, but the Irish were one of only two undefeated teams. (Ohio State, on probation, was the other.) They also had the nation's No. 1 scoring defense.

While the Tide coaches and players were cautious leading up to the game, they were also confident. Offensive tackle D.J. Fluker said that in the locker room before the game, "the mindset [was] that we were going to come out here and dominate."

That domination began with an immediate fast start. Alabama needed less than three minutes to score. Junior running back Eddie Lacy, the game's most valuable offensive player, broke off a 20-yard touchdown run. That quick score was clearly an early sign that Notre Dame was in for a long night.

After an Irish punt, Alabama raced downfield, covering 61 yards in ten plays. A 3-yard pass from A.J. McCarron to tight end

Michael Williams ended the drive. It was quickly 14-0.

By halftime, the rout was on with Alabama leading 28-0. Interviewed at the break, Irish head coach Brian Kelly admitted that about the only way his team could turn the game around was if the Crimson Tide didn't come out in the second half. But they did, and they came out fast, covering 97 yards in ten plays to lead 35-0.

Thanks in part to the fast start from which the Irish never recovered, the Tide romped to a 42-14 win and the national title.

Fast starts are crucial for more than football games and races. Any time we begin something new, we want to get out of the gate quickly and jump ahead of the pack and stay there. As the Tide did against Notre Dame, we build up momentum from a fast start and keep rolling.

This is true for our faith life also. For a time after we accepted Christ as our savior, we were on fire with a zeal that wouldn't let us rest, much like the early Christians described in Acts. All too many Christians, however, let that blaze die down until only old ashes remain. We become lukewarm pew sitters.

The Christian life shouldn't be that way. Just because we were tepid yesterday doesn't mean we can't be boiling today. Every day we can turn to God for a spiritual tune-up that will put a new spark in our faith life; with a little tending that spark can soon become a raging fire. Today could be the day our faith life gets off to a fast start — again.

We came out, started fast and finished strong like we always preach.
— A.J. McCarron on the BCS win over Notre Dame

**Every day offers us yet another chance
to get off to a fast start for Jesus.**

DAY 11

GOOD IDEA

Read Luke 8:40-56.

"In the presence of all the people, she told why she had touched him" (v. 47).

Fred Sington had what turned out to be a really good idea, even if it was downright weird.

An All-American senior tackle on the 1930 squad that went undefeated and won the national title, Sington was so famous that legendary singer Rudy Vallee celebrated his gridiron abilities with the song "Football Freddie." It became a national hit. Notre Dame coach Knute Rockne called Sington "the greatest lineman in the country."

As a freshman in 1927, Sington came up with an idea that led directly to a win for the team of rookies. Against their first-year counterparts from Georgia, the Tide freshmen wound up tied 7-7 at halftime. As Sington put it, "We were pretty ragged."

Coach Clyde "Shorty" Propst was so upset with his charges that he wouldn't let them go into the dressing room at the break. Instead, Sington said, "He took us over under some bleachers and he was giving us down the country about how we were playing."

The players just quietly looked at each other while their coach chewed them out. That is, until Sington interrupted Propst by asking if he could speak. He said he had an idea that might turn the game around.

Sington pointed out that for the past two weeks the freshman team had run Georgia's plays at practice to prepare the varsity defense for the upcoming game against the Bulldogs. Sington said they hadn't run their plays in so long they had almost forgotten them. So he proposed that they run Georgia's plays the last half.

With nothing to lose, Propst went along with the rather bizarre idea. The result, interestingly enough, was three quick second-half touchdowns "and a one-sided victory" for the freshmen.

The good ideas we have may not win a Tide football game but they nevertheless shape our lives for the better. You've probably had a few moments of inspiration, divine or otherwise, yourself. Attending Alabama or becoming a Crimson Tide fan, marrying that person you did, maybe going back to school or starting a business or a family — they were good ideas.

From climbing aboard a horse's back to anesthesia to Double Stuf Oreos, good ideas are nothing new. The trouble is they're usually pretty hard to come by — except for the one that is right there before us all.

That woman with the bleeding problem had it. So did Jarius, the synagogue ruler. They had a big problem in their lives, so they came up with the notion that they should turn to Jesus and trust in him for help, hope, and deliverance.

It was a good idea then; it's a good idea now, the best ever, in fact. Surrendering your life to Jesus is such a good idea that its effects reverberate through all eternity.

Let's try it.
— *Coach Shorty Propst's reply to Fred Sington's crazy idea*

**Good ideas are hard to come by except for
the best idea of all: giving your life to Jesus.**

DAY 12

LEAD THE WAY

Read Judges 6:1-6, 11-16.

"'But Lord,' Gideon asked, 'how can I save Israel? My clan is the weakest . . . and I am the least in my family'" (v 15).

She gave pep talks to her team. She helped a teammate work on her swing. She offered fielding tips to a freshman. An Alabama coach? Nope. Senior Charlotte Morgan, the ultimate leader.

As a senior in 2010 on Alabama's softball team, Morgan was the SEC Player of the Year for the second time. She hit .350, was 7-2 as a pitcher, and led the team with 16 home runs. She set an SEC record with 264 career RBIs. She was All-America three times.

The lone senior on the field, Morgan was the undisputed leader of the 2010 team. Even the coaches recognized it. For instance, assistant coach Alyson Habetz suggested that Morgan work with sophomore Jennifer Fenton when she dropped into a batting slump. Morgan "just has that respect," Habetz explained. Her teammates "listen, absolutely."

On the field, Morgan played first base when she wasn't pitching, and she kept up a running dialogue of support for the player throwing for the Tide. "I know kind of exactly what to say to get into her head," Morgan said about helping out her mound mate.

She offered teammates encouragement when they made errors in the field. For instance, freshman Kayla Braud found herself playing second base for the first time ever. "Every single inning, she's talking to me, helping me out, she's giving me tips and stuff," Braud said of Morgan. "Without her, I don't know if I could have pulled it off at all."

And just how did that squad do under Morgan's leadership? Quite nicely indeed. They finished the season at 52-11 as both SEC and SEC tournament champions. Ranked in the top ten, they advanced to a Super Regional in the NCAA Tournament.

Over and over in the Bible, God anoints the unlikeliest people to be leaders in accomplishing the divine purpose. Gideon, for instance, was a nobody from a nothing group, cowering in fear of his people's powerful enemies. Even he protested he was poor leadership material.

But that didn't matter to God. "I will be you with you," was God's answer, and that settled the matter.

This pattern God employs should give us all pause. Just as it was back with the oppressed Israelites centuries ago, God still needs leaders working for the advancement of his kingdom. And just as folks like Gideon, Moses, and Jeremiah did, you probably can come up with what you believe to be reasons why that leader shouldn't be you.

Here's the unsettling truth: Even for you, those reasons don't matter to God. The determining factor is still God's declaration, "I will be with you." So, lead the way, confident you are not alone. God's kingdom needs leaders; if you don't lead, who will?

I couldn't have asked for a better senior leader.
— Second baseman Kayla Braud on Charlotte Morgan

Just as he always has, God needs leaders;
God needs you.

DAY 13

RUN FOR IT

Read John 20:1-10.

"Peter and the other disciple started for the tomb. Both were running, but the other disciple outran Peter and reached the tomb first" (vv. 3-4).

Shaun Alexander called his own number. The coaches listened, and when he finished running, the Tide had a legendary upset.

From 1996-99, Alexander, a running back, set fifteen school records including career rushing yards (3,565) and most rushing yards in a game (291 against LSU in 1996). Speculation was widespread that he would turn pro after his junior season, but he decided to return to Tuscaloosa. Among his reasons was his desire to use his position in the spotlight "to share God's love with as many people, especially young people, as I can."

Eminently quotable, Alexander once said that when he ran behind All-American tackle Chris Samuels and got to the line of scrimmage, "There's usually one dead body or two badly injured guys or three guys wounded on the ground. It just depends on what kind of mood Chris is in."

Thus, when it came time for one of the biggest plays of the 1999 season, Alexander knew exactly what the offense should do. It should run him behind Samuels.

Alabama would win the SEC in '99, but the Tide was an underdog in Gainesville on Oct. 2. The Gators were 4-0, ranked No. 3, and had won thirty straight games in The Swamp.

The game was a classic. With 1:25 left, Alexander scored from the 13 on fourth-and-one to tie the game at 33. Florida scored in the overtime but missed the extra point.

Alexander had a play in mind he was convinced he would score on. He ran up to assistant coach Ivy Williams and said they should run a counter to Samuels' left. Williams called the press box and got the OK.

Alexander had it right. Behind blocks from Samuels and tight end Shawn Draper, he bolted into the end zone on the first play. Chris Kemp's PAT finished off the monumental 40-39 upset.

Hit the ground running — every morning that's what you do as you leave the house and re-enter the rat race. You run errands; you run though a presentation; you give someone a run for his money; you always want to be in the running and never run-of-the-mill.

You're always running toward something, such as your goals, or away from something, such as your past. Many of us spend much of our lives attempting to run away from God, the purposes he has for us, and the blessings he is waiting to give us.

No matter how hard or how far you run, though, you can never outrun yourself or God. God keeps pace with you, calling you in the short run to take care of the long run by falling to your knees and running for your life — to Jesus — just as Peter and the other disciple ran that first Easter morning.

On your knees, you run all the way to glory.

Don't go down and we've got the game won.
— Shaun Alexander to himself on his run that beat Florida in '99

You can run to eternity by going to your knees.

DAY 14

JUST PERFECT

Read Matthew 5:43-48.

"Be perfect, therefore, as your heavenly Father is perfect"
(v. 48).

In the 2014 Iron Bowl, Alabama was a mess, far from perfect. All the Tide did was win.

A one-sided look at the game's statistics declares that there was no way Alabama could have beaten the 15th-ranked Tigers. The Tide turned the ball over three times. They fell behind early by twelve points. The defense was a wide-open faucet, surrendering an incredible 630 yards of offense. After the game, head coach Nick Saban proclaimed the first half to be "about as bad a half of football as we've played all year."

And yet, the final score was 55-44, Alabama, a win that sent the team to the SEC title game. The Red Elephants won despite their mistakes, despite their imperfections. After the game, Saban said his team seems "to always be able to be resilient enough to play through adversity, which we certainly did today."

ESPN's Ivan Maisel called the 2014 college football season "the year of the flawed"; thus, he said, "Alabama might be the ideal No. 1," as demonstrated by the Iron Bowl.

So how did the Tide win? For one thing, Alabama rolled up 539 yards of its own. Amari Cooper, a unanimous All-America and the winner of the Fred Biletnikoff Award as the nation's top wide receiver, tied his own school record with 224 yards receiving. T.J.

Yeldon rushed for 127 yards and two touchdowns.

But Alabama ultimately won because of its dominance of the red zone. Inside the Alabama 20, the beleaguered defense was at its best. Auburn made the trip eight times but could manage only two touchdowns and five field goals. Alabama made it into the end zone on each of its five excursions inside the Auburn 20.

In that one vital part of the game, Alabama was perfect.

Football teams are never perfect and neither are people. We botch our personal relationships; at work we seek competence, not perfection. To insist upon personal or professional perfection in our lives is to establish an impossibly high standard that will eventually destroy us physically, emotionally, and mentally.

Yet that is exactly the standard God sets for us. Our love is to be perfect, never ceasing, never failing, never qualified – just the way God loves us. And Jesus didn't limit his command to only preachers and goody-two-shoes types. All of his disciples are to be perfect as they navigate their way through the world's ambiguous definition and understanding of love.

But that's impossible! Well, not necessarily, if to love perfectly is to serve God wholeheartedly and to follow Jesus with single-minded devotion. Anyhow, in his perfect love for us, God makes allowance for our imperfect love and the consequences of it in the perfection of Jesus.

We misexecuted a lot of things.
— Nick Saban, describing his team's play vs. Auburn in 2014

**In his perfect love for us, God provides a way
for us to escape the consequences of
our imperfect love for him: Jesus.**

DAY 15

GREAT EXPECTATIONS

Read John 1:43-51.

"'Nazareth! Can anything good come from there?'
Nathanael asked" (v. 46).

The coaches had no idea what to expect when Gary Hollingsworth became the team's starting quarterback.

Hollingsworth was more interested in pitching a baseball than throwing a football. His development as a quarterback at Alabama was hampered by that interest in baseball because he was excused from spring practice to pitch for the Tide nine. The absence meant that as his junior season of 1989 approached, he had never taken a varsity snap and thus was relegated to backup duty behind senior Jeff Dunn.

Hollingsworth was described as a tall, skinny kid, an image that was borne out by the combination of his height (tall at 6 ft. 4 in.) and his weight (thin at 187 lbs.). Offensive coordinator Homer Smith once described his approach to lifting weights as "reluctant." Strength coach Rich Wingo struggled to put some weight on the backup quarterback, leading Smith to say, "Gary doesn't eat real seriously." Once when the trainer asked Hollingsworth if he needed anything, he replied, "Yeah. Twenty pounds."

As quarterbacks go, he was slow. Asked once to run a 40-yard dash, he responded, "Does it all have to be in one day?" One writer said, the "hole doesn't exist that can open long enough for Hollingsworth to meander through it."

Thus, the expectations were that Hollingsworth would see only limited action during the '89 season. That changed in a hurry when Dunn went down with an injury in the second game. The team's reluctant quarterback was now the starter.

Hollingsworth more than exceeded expectations. In his fourth game, a 47-30 win over undefeated Tennessee, he set a school record with 32 completions. He led the Tide to ten straight wins, a Sugar-Bowl berth, and a No. 9 national ranking. He made All-SEC.

The blind date your friend promised would look just like Ryan Reynolds or Jennifer Lawrence but instead resembled Cousin Itt or an extra in a zombie flick. Your vacation that went downhill after the lost luggage. Often your expectations are raised only to be dashed. Sometimes it's best not to get your hopes up; then at least you have the possibility of being surprised.

Worst of all, perhaps, is when you realize that you are the one not meeting others' expectations. The fact is, though, that you aren't here to live up to what others think of you. Jesus didn't; in part, that's why they killed him. But he did meet God's expectations for his life, which was all that really mattered.

Because God's kingdom is so great, God does have great expectations for any who would enter, and you should not take them lightly. What the world expects from you is of no importance; what God expects from you is paramount.

Gary Hollingsworth continues to amaze me.
— Tide head coach Bill Curry, perhaps not expecting much

You have little if anything to gain from meeting the world's expectations of you; you have all of eternity to gain from meeting God's.

DAY 16

NOTHING DOING

Read Hebrews 10:19-25.

"[L]et us consider how we may spur one another on toward love and good deeds. . . . [L]et us encourage one another" (vv. 24, 25b).

Ultimately, Wimp Sanderson couldn't hide anymore. His teams were just too good for him to remain anonymous.

Sanderson started his career at Alabama in total anonymity in 1960 as a graduate assistant to Hayden Riley. "To tell the truth, I had only planned to stay for one year," he once said. Instead, the following year he was named to head coach C.M. Newton's staff and held that position for twenty years.

Newton left for Vanderbilt in 1980 and recommended to athletic director Bear Bryant that he name Sanderson the new head coach. Bryant did. When Sanderson went to the Bear to thank him for the chance, Bryant growled, "Wimp, I didn't have nothing to do with it. But I sure could've stopped it if I wanted to."

And so the no-name, but savvy, assistant become the no-name, but savvier, head coach at Alabama. He also had seemed to land a one-way ticket to anonymity at a school whose fan base believed the head football coach walked on water while the other coaches were around to tote the buckets.

It didn't turn out that way. Before long, people began to notice that Sanderson was about the serious business of making the Tide a part of the national college basketball landscape. He averaged more than 22 wins a season during his 12-year tenure in Tuscaloosa, and his teams made ten trips to the NCAA Tournament. He was the National Coach of the Year in 1987 and was inducted into the Alabama Sports Hall of Fame in 1990.

Everybody found out who Wimp Sanderson was.

Successful, big-time college coaches such as Wimp Sanderson don't labor in anonymity very long. In contrast, Christians humbly and steadfastly serving their Lord — especially in their local church — typically remain rather anonymous. Their glory is found in their service, not in vaingloriously seeking out the praise of others.

For all too many Christians, however, the form of anonymity they choose is not what God has in mind. They're the ones who come to church — perhaps faithfully — and then go home, maybe feeling quite smug after dropping an extra $20 in the collection plate. They just show up, sit, maybe mumble the words to a hymn or two, and listen to at least part of the sermon. That's it. They are no-names and do-nothings.

That is not the kind of faith life Christ calls us to. As Hebrews tells us, we are to confidently and assuredly help and encourage others on their faith journey. We are to serve God so that both other Christians and non-believers know our names and that we are people of faith.

If we live that way, God, too, will know our name.

I was a no-name coach. I guess I still am.
— *Wimp Sanderson*

**Anonymity for the Christian is found
in service, not in doing nothing.**

DAY 17

A GOOD IMPRESSION

Read John 1:1-18.

"In the beginning was the Word, and the Word was with God, and the Word was God. . . . The Word became flesh and made his dwelling among us" (vv. 1, 14).

Dont'a Hightower made quite a first impression on Nick Saban.

Hightower was apparently destined to be a mechanic. At least, that was his grandfather's plans. Hightower grew up in rural Tennessee, spending hours with his grandfather tinkering with cars in the garage. His grandfather was preparing him for a career.

That all changed the first time the youngster put on the pads and stepped onto a football field. Hightower was "a once-in-a-generation, two-way player," his high school team's starting tailback and its middle linebacker.

Just as football made an indelible impression on Hightower the first time he got involved with it, so did Hightower made an indelible first impression on the Tide's head coach. Saban made the trip himself to Lewisburg, Tenn., to see what all the fuss was about. He went in the spring, so he didn't have a chance to see Hightower in a game.

It didn't matter. Saban watched the junior go through various drills on the first day of spring practice 2007. Hightower noticed a man on the sideline watching him, but he didn't recognize the Alabama coach. Saban was so impressed that within hours after that one-time practice he called Hightower and offered him a scholarship. "I was blown away," Saban said. "What I saw that day in the indoor practice facility at his school was probably the most athletic linebacker in the country."

Hightower was a freshman All-American linebacker in 2008. He returned in 2010 from a gruesome injury to his left knee that cost him most of the 2009 season and was a first-team All-American in 2011. He then turned pro.

That fetching person in the apartment next door. A job search that comes complete with interview. A class reunion. The new neighbors. We are constantly about the fraught task of wanting to make an impression on people. We want them to remember us, obviously in a flattering way, which means we probably should be circumspect in our personal conduct.

We make that impression, good or bad, generally in two ways. Even with instant communication on the Internet — perhaps especially with the Internet — we primarily influence the opinion others have of us by our words. After that, we can advance to the next level by making an impression with our actions.

God gave us an impression of himself in exactly the same way. In Jesus, God took the unprecedented step of appearing to mortals as one of us, as mere flesh and bone. We now know for all time the sorts of things God does and the sorts of things God says. In Jesus, God put his divine foot forward to make a good impression on each one of us.

I knew right away he could be a perfect fit for what we wanted to do.
— Nick Saban on his first impression of Dont'a Hightower

Through Jesus' words and actions,
God seeks to impress us with his love.

DAY 18

HEART STRINGS

Read John 9:17-36.

"When Jesus saw [Mary] weeping, . . . he was deeply moved in spirit and troubled" (v. 33).

Terrence Cody didn't feel one tiny bit of remorse or sympathy because he had helped reduce Tim Tebow to tears.

"Mount Cody" is part of Alabama lore. Standing 6'5" and tipping the scales at 354 lbs. (after weighing 410 lbs. at junior college), Cody was a two-time All-American nosetackle for the Tide (2008 and '09).

His senior year in high school, Cody weighed in at 405 lbs. and could dunk a basketball. His coaches had to install The Terrence Rule, which forbade him from tackling his teammates in practice. The rule resulted from the first day in pads when Cody tackled a teammate who weighed about 145 lbs. The head coach said Cody "land[ed] square on top of [the kid]. All I can see is a foot — and it's moving, so I know he isn't dead." During a play after the rule was instituted, Cody lifted the fullback onto his shoulder, walked over to his head coach, and asked, "Is this good enough?"

The 2009 SEC Championship Game featured a rematch of the '08 game won by the Gators and their Heisman-Trophy winning quarterback, who went on to win the national title. The '09 dream game featured two 12-0 teams with the winner heading for the BCS championship game (won by the Tide vs. Texas).

CRIMSON TIDE

The game was not the thriller everybody expected as Alabama drubbed Florida 32-13. The Tide reduced "Tebow to tears and otherwise [bullied] the national champions." Those tears first showed up during the last minute of the game. Unsympathetic Alabama fans cheered, and Cody was right there with them.

"For us to dominate him . . . it meant a lot to us," he said.

While we don't expect cruelty on the football field, we don't expect sympathy for the opponent either. Sportsmanship is what is called for.

Our games, however, are an exception to the general way we are to live as modeled by Jesus himself. Our Lord was moved to tears by the grief of Lazarus' family. His example should lead us to a life of sympathy and compassion, not stoicism and indifference. But as Jesus did, we are to move beyond mere commiseration; we are to act, to do what we can to alleviate another person's misery.

In this fallen, cursed world, the needs are overwhelming. Even Jesus didn't eradicate disease, hunger, misery, or suffering. We can't either. That's no reason, however, for us to just sit down, wail about how bad everything is, and impertinently ask God why he doesn't do something about all this mess. His response to that question is an obvious one: he will ask each of us the same question.

We are to love our neighbor. That love reveals itself when sympathy and compassion spur us into action.

Our standard was to be as good as Florida. Today, we were better.
— Tide linebacker Cory Reamer, showing no sympathy

**Jesus wept and then took action to meet a need;
we are to do nothing less.**

DAY 19

BEYOND THE PAST

Read Colossians 3:1-10.

"You used to walk in these ways, in the life you once lived. But now you must rid yourself of all such things" (vv. 7, 8a).

When Alabama met Georgia Tech in 1964, two-platoon football was brand new, the Yellow Jackets had just left the SEC, and Bear Bryant had won only one national title. It was a different age, that time in the past.

The Tide and the Jackets haven't played since 1984. Back in '64, though, the teams had played every season since 1922 except for a four-year break from 1942-46. Back then, the team had to fly to Atlanta on two twin-engine planes since the Tuscaloosa airport couldn't accommodate four-engine planes or jets.

The Bear was 51, but even then rumors persisted that he was ready to retire. His wife, Mary, who died in 1984, declared that such a rumor "just naturally gets started at recruitin' time by those old Aubuhn people."

Senior Joe Namath and junior Steve Sloan were the quarterbacks back then in 1964. Sloan stepped in when Namath suffered a knee injury. A tackler in the Vanderbilt game (whch Bama won 24-0), jeered at Namath, "Hey, No. 12, what's your name?" "You'll see it in the headlines tomorrow," Namath replied. On the next play, he threw a touchdown pass.

Football was so different back then that Bryant was leery of the new two-platoon football. He declared he was glad to see the Tech series end because Tech recruited better than Alabama did and thus, "Tech would beat us four out of five times."

Pre-game pep rallies were held in the gymnasium back then. The crowd brought garbage-can covers and shouted "Steve Sloan for President."

One thing for sure wasn't different back then: Alabama won. The Tide beat the Jackets 24-7 on the way to a 10-0 season and the national championship (Associated Press).

The past often seems quaint to us. It's difficult for us to imagine Alabama football as it was more than fifty years ago in 1964.

But in our personal lives, the past usually isn't quaint at all. Instead, it often haunts us like a ghost. We lug around our regrets and memories of our past failures, omissions, and shortcomings, donning them each day as we do our clothes.

Short of utter callousness and severe memory problems, only one way exists to free ourselves totally from the past: the change offered through salvation in Jesus Christ. Even when we fall on our knees in despair and cry out to Jesus, we sometimes falsely believe that salvation and forgiveness can never be ours. That's because many desperate seekers fall prey to the fallacy that they must be perfect before Jesus will accept them. The truth is that we need Jesus because we are not perfect.

Jesus didn't die for our past but for our future. He died to free us from the past and to replace it with a glorious future.

Make the present good, and the past will take care of itself.
— *Knute Rockne*

Every saint has a past; every sinner has a future.

BEYOND THE PAST   39

DAY 20

AUTHORITY FIGURE

Read Psalm 95:1-7a.

"Come, let us bow down in worship, let us kneel before the Lord" (v. 6).

After his first-ever scrimmage, A.J. McCarron questioned Nick Saban's authority. It didn't go too well.

McCarron's legacy at Alabama is secure. He quarterbacked the Tide to back-to-back national titles (2011, 2012) and holds the school records for wins and for career passing yards.

McCarron came to Tuscaloosa, however, as something less than a star recruit. "It was entirely possible he would never start a game," said assistant athletic director Tommy Ford.

Thus, he was grouped with the walk-ons for his first-ever intrasquad scrimmage in 2009. As expected, the defensive starters sacked him early, late, and often. McCarron wasn't at all happy about it. In fact, he didn't even stop to take off his cleats before he stormed into Saban's office after the practice.

"I need to talk to you," he snapped. "Okay," Saban apparently quite calmly replied.

"You want me to show you what I can do, how I can play?" McCarron thundered. "I can't do [anything] when you put me with walk-ons who can't even block. I don't understand why you don't put me with the [starters]."

Saban didn't really even look up from his desk. "Because today we were testing your leadership," the head coach replied. "And you failed. Miserably."

After that rocky beginning, McCarron eventually became "the ideal extension of Saban on the field." Saban even agreed with his quarterback's declaration that he was closer to his head coach than to any other adults except his parents. The relationship was so close that even the assistant coaches leaned on McCarron to ask Saban for favors. "You're the only one he listens to," one coach lamented.

But it sure didn't start out that way, that day McCarron challenged Saban and got his comeuppance.

Stand up for yourself. Be your own person. Cherish your independence. That's what the world tells us. Naively, we may believe it and plan to live just that way — until we grow up and discover that authority figures don't take kindly to being challenged by those under their supervision or direction. Our basic survival skills kick in, and we change our tune: play along, don't rock the boat, be a company person. We become — gasp! — obedient, dampening our rebelliousness for a greater purpose.

Our relationship with God is similar in that he demands obedience from us. We believe in and trust what Jesus told us as the revealed word of God, and then we are obedient to it.

Obedience — even to God — is not easy for us. It vexes us, at least until we learn that what we surrender in independence to God is meaningless compared to the blessings we gain in return.

Coming in as an 18-year-old, I probably – definitely – wasn't the wisest.
— A.J. McCarron on challenging Nick Saban early on

God seeks our obedience out of a loving desire to provide us with rich, purposeful, and joyous lives.

DAY 21

A HEX ON YOU

Read Jonah 1.

"Tell us, who is responsible for making all this trouble for us? What did you do?" (v. 8a)

Following a time-honored softball tradition, the Alabama players wouldn't say a word about what was happening. They didn't want to jinx it.

Not until the fourth inning did Tide softball head coach Patrick Murphy look down at his scorecard and realize that sophomore pitcher Sydney Littlejohn was about the business of making some history. The occasion was the second game of the 2015 season, a match-up against Eastern Kentucky in the Sand Dollar Classic.

"I looked at the score sheet to see what a girl had done, and it was 1-2-3, 1-2-3, 1-2-3," Murphy said. "I was like, 'Man, she has a no-hitter.'" But it was more than that; it was a perfect game.

As she took the mound to pitch the fourth inning, Littlejohn realized the same thing. She then understood the obvious: Her teammates weren't saying a word to her out of fear they might jinx her. So Littlejohn didn't talk about it either.

Watching closely in the dugout was pitching coach Stephanie VanBrakle. On April 1, 2006, she threw the program's first perfect game in a win over Kentucky. She was so dialed in to calling the pitches, however, that she didn't catch on to the perfect game until it was over. Littlejohn set down the next six batters in order to complete an 8-0 run-rule perfect game and the win.

"I kept the lineup card," Littlejohn said later about making a piece of Alabama softball history. "I already have it framed."

Littlejohn's place in history got quite a bit larger exactly one month later. On March 6, she became the first Tide pitcher ever to toss two perfect games. Behind Littlejohn's perfect and jinx-free pitching, the Tide rolled past Ole Miss 10-0.

Hexes and jinxes may be fun on the softball field, but elsewhere they belong to the domain of superstitious balderdash.

Some people do feel, however, that they exist under a dark and rainy cloud. Nothing goes right; all their dreams collapse around them; they seem to constantly bring about misery on themselves and also on the ones around them.

Why? Is it really a hex, a jinx?

Nonsense. The Bible provides us an excellent example in Jonah. The sailors on the boat with the reluctant prophet believed him to be a hex and the source of their bad luck. Jonah's life was a mess, but it had nothing to do with any jinx. His life was in shambles because he was disobeying God.

Take a careful look at people you know whose lives are in shambles, including some who profess to believe in God. The key to life lies not in belief alone; the responsibility of the believer is to obey God. Problems never have their root in hexes, but all too often their source is disobedience.

It was one of those things you try not to think about because once you start thinking about it, it gets jinxed.
— Sydney Littlejohn on her perfect game vs. Eastern Kentucky

Hexes don't cause us trouble,
but disobedience to God sure does.

DAY 22

MEMORY LOSS

Read 1 Corinthians 11:17-29.

"[D]o this in remembrance of me" (v. 24).

The memory of the night that he failed his mama drove Amari Cooper to football excellence.

A wide receiver, Cooper headed to the pros following his junior season of 2014. On his way to winning awards and All-American plaudits, he set Alabama career records for receiving yards (3,463), receptions (228), and touchdown catches (31). He helped the Tide win two SEC titles and a national championship (2012).

The whole time, he never stopped working. *SI*'s Andy Staples wrote, "While other players are sleeping or partying, Alabama wideout Amai Cooper is getting in extra workouts." His regular routine included early mornings and late nights in the weight room, "two workouts on days in which some of the best athletes in college football struggled to finish one."

Cooper finished third among the Heisman finalists in 2014. At the trophy ceremony in New York City, he gave the world a glimpse into what drives him so relentlessly. He did it by relating a story about one night when he was a teenager.

His mother, Michelle Green, who was beside him on the Heisman stage, had come home after working all day. She still had to walk three miles one way to the supermarket to buy food. She asked Cooper to go with her to help her carry the bags. He said he couldn't; he was too tired.

So she made the trip alone. When she finally made it home, she had marks on her arms left by the heavy bags on the long walk. How tired was *she*, Cooper asked in New York City. She, he said, who never complained while she raised three children and two nephews working as a cashier and a waitress.

His mother had long since forgotten all about that night, but Cooper remembered those stripes, his behavior, and his guilt. So he emulated his mother and how hard she worked for him.

Memory makes us who we are. Whether our memories appear as pleasant reverie or unnerving nightmares, they shape us and to a large extent determine both our actions and our reactions. Alzheimer's is so terrifying because it steals our memory from us, and in the process we lose ourselves. We disappear.

The greatest tragedy of our lives is that God remembers. In response to that photographic memory, he condemns us for our sin. Paradoxically, the greatest joy of our lives is that God remembers. In response to that memory, he came as Jesus to wash even the memory of our sins away.

God uses memory as a tool through which we encounter revival. At the Last Supper, Jesus instructed his disciples and us to remember. In sharing this unique meal with fellow believers and remembering Jesus and his actions, we meet Christ again, not just as a memory but as an actual living presence. To remember is to keep our faith alive.

I'm still kind of feeding off of that.
— *Amari Cooper, recalling the night he was 'too tired' to help his mama*

Because we remember Jesus,
God will not remember our sins.

DAY 23

CLUELESS

Read Matthew 16:21-23.

"[Y]ou do not have in mind the things of God, but the things of men" (v. 23b).

Safety Mike Clements was in on the most legendary play in Alabama football history. Before that happened, though, he was so bad his position coach described him as clueless.

An iconic *Sports Illustrated* photograph and Daniel Moore's painting titled "The Goal Line Stand" have preserved the fourth-down tackle at the six-inch line in the 1979 Sugar Bowl against Penn State. (See Devotion No. 68.) For some inexplicable reason, Clements' role in the play has been largely forgotten.

In the photo and in Moore's painting, Clements appears as half a helmet, No. 43, that is planted in the side of Penn State's running back. He kept the back from jumping over the pile and thus gave other tacklers time to get to the ball carrier.

Clements might well not have been on the field at all. He got his first chance to show what he could do in 1978 as a redshirt sophomore. He was awful. In the first game of the season, he fell down and gave up a long pass. "From then on," he remembered, "I'm afraid to get on the football field."

It got worse. "I [felt] like I didn't want to play football," he said. He was ready to quit. Defensive assistant coach Bill Oliver said Clements "was absolutely just clueless." Instead of giving up on Clements, though, Oliver gave him a wake-up call one day at practice. "Coaches don't usually touch players," Clements recalled, but "I'm daydreaming . . . and he comes over and grabs my facemask." He yelled at Clements to get his backside in gear.

Clements realized Oliver didn't think he could play and was shocked into proving his coach wrong. He did, and the clueless safety became part of Alabama gridiron history.

Clueless. It's one of our age's most venomous insults. It's an interesting word in that it is its own oxymoron. People are clueless only when they do indeed have the clues at hand and still don't get it. It's not to be confused with ignorance, which occurs when people don't have access to facts, figures, and information.

From the desert-dwelling Israelites grumbling about Moses and God to the Pharisees and other religious leaders of Jesus' day, the Bible is replete with the clueless. Simon Peter, who had all the clues he needed standing right in front of his face, drew a soul-searing rebuke from Jesus for being clueless.

The Bible remains relevant and timeless because centuries after it was compiled, human nature hasn't changed one bit. As it was in Jesus' time, people who have heard the Gospel may still be divided into the clued-in and the clueless: those who get it and those who don't.

Fortunately for the clueless, they can always change groups as Peter did. They can affirm Jesus as their savior and surrender their lives to him. They need you as a witness to clue them in.

I made my share of mistakes — over and over again.
— Mike Clements on being clueless

**Clueless or clued-in is a matter of whether
you have given your life to Jesus.**

DAY 24

DO WHAT YOU MUST

Read 2 Samuel 12:1-15a.

"The Lord sent Nathan to David" (v. 1).

His parents told Baxter Booth he couldn't quit, so he did whatever it took to survive.

Bear Bryant's first spring training camp in Tuscaloosa was in 1958. As he had done in 1954 at Texas A&M, Bryant set out in a three-month long "spring" training to find out which guys really wanted to play football. It started in January, and rising senior tackle Chuck Allen said simply, "It was brutal."

During two-a-days, there were no water breaks. "The kind of jerseys they had for us you could have worn in Siberia," remembered Tommy Brooker, a freshman end who played on the 1961 national champions. He said that the players would ball the jerseys up to allow for some breathing room. Then when the sweat collected there, "we'd suck on it." For Brooker, the most bizarre moment came when he felt a tug from behind. Another player was sucking the sweat out of his jersey.

Bryant saw the rising seniors as responsible for a lot of Alabama's losses. He dropped them all, including Allen and Booth, an offensive end, to the last team. Discouraged and sapped by the grueling practices, they decided to quit.

Back home in Athens ostensibly for the weekend, Booth needed a while to work up the nerve to tell his parents he was giving up football. Their reply was blunt. "You ain't giving it up," they said.

"Get your fanny back down there."

Booth did and so did Allen. They both did whatever it took to survive that spring. When Allen suffered a concussion in practice one day, he had to wait in the back of a station wagon until they got a full load to be hauled to the hospital. It didn't take long. Allen was kept overnight, and he said, "I can't tell you how happy I was to be in that hospital."

Booth and Allen did what they had to, survived spring training, and started for Bama and the Bear in the fall.

Like those players in '58, you've had to do some things in your life that you really didn't want to do. Maybe when you put your daughter on severe restriction, broke the news of a death in the family, fired a friend, or underwent surgery. You plowed ahead because you knew it was for the best or you had no choice.

Nathan surely didn't want to confront King David and tell him what a miserable reprobate he'd been, but the prophet had no choice: Obedience to God overrode all other factors. Of all that God asks of us in the living of a godly life, obedience is perhaps the most difficult. After all, our history of disobedience stretches all the way back to the Garden of Eden.

The problem is that God expects obedience not only when his wishes match our own but also when they don't. Obedience to God is a way of life, not a matter of convenience.

The big guy couldn't get me in there.
— Chuck Allen on the relief of staying overnight in the hospital

You can never foresee what God will demand
of you, but obedience requires being ready
to do whatever God asks.

THE CARETAKERS

Read Genesis 1:20-28.

"Rule over the fish of the sea and the birds of the air and over every living creature that moves on the ground" (v. 28b).

For years, the Alabama golf teams had a four-legged member of the squads. Her name was Jerry.

Jerry was a tabby cat who became the teams' unofficial mascot in 2007. Men's coach Jay Seawall said he was walking outside the Jerry Pate Golf Complex during the summer when he heard a cat meow. He found Jerry underneath the golf team's van. She was "just a scraggly stray."

Seawall brought Jerry inside and she never left until her death in April 2015. Her main job was to catch the field mice who frequently scampered through the golf complex, and she was very good at it.

It wasn't all work and no play for Jerry the cat, though. She would often steal unguarded golf balls. She liked to nap in any open locker she could find. Women's golf coach Mic Potter said her favorite spots for sleeping were in his office, either on a shelf or on his computer keyboard.

Jerry liked to be with the players when they were on the greens outside. She would sit next to the golfers as they teed off, sometimes swatting at the balls or rubbing their legs. The players never seemed to mind and weren't distracted by her antics.

Jerry also liked to hang out with the players when they were inside the complex. Seawall said she would sit on the couch with the team members when they were watching television.

After Jerry was sick for a few weeks with what was probably cancer, Seawall and the team made the difficult decision to put her down. "She was a good pet around here," he said. "She leaves with five SEC titles and three national championships, which isn't a bad run for a cat."

The affection the Alabama golf teams had for Jerry and the care they heaped upon her serve as excellent illustrations for a task God has delegated to us. God paused after each step of his creation to assess what he had done. Inevitably, he was pleased with it and declared it "good." That included the animals.

After God had stocked the planet with plants, animals, and fish, he created humankind. He then appointed us the rulers of his creation, particularly the living things. To rule is to have absolute authority. So it is with us and God's creation.

In declaring us to be rulers, God took the step of ensuring his creation would be taken care of. Overall, we've done a pretty miserable job of it.

That's because God gave us the freedom to decide what kind of ruler we will be. We can be despots wielding our power cruelly and heartlessly. Or we can be benevolent autocrats who use our authority to protect and to care for — as God does for us.

She's kind of a mascot, a very viable part of what Alabama golf is.
— Men's golf coach Jay Seawall on Jerry the cat

**We will answer to God for
how we have cared for his creation.**

DAY 26

OBSTACLE COURSE

Read 2 Corinthians 12:23-33.

"I have been in prison more frequently, been flogged more severely, and been exposed to death again and again" (v. 23b).

Not big enough. Small school. Injured. Disrespected. Brodie Croyle knows all about obstacles.

He played in high school for a small Christian academy. He was 6-2 but he weighed less than 200 pounds, just too skinny. He missed his senior season with a knee injury. Still, he brushed all those obstacles aside and landed a scholarship to Alabama. That may well be when the serious obstacles really started.

Croyle came to Tuscaloosa in 2002 and played during perhaps the most tumultuous period in Alabama football history. The program was hit with probation and had one coach for two seasons, another for four months, and a third who was a first-time head man. Amid all that turmoil, Croyle tore the ACL in his right knee and was out for most of his junior season.

Despite all the obstacles, Croyle excelled. He completed his Alabama career in 2005 as the most prolific passer in Crimson Tide history. He left Tuscaloosa owning just about every passing and total offense record in the book.

His last game for Alabama was the 2006 Cotton Bowl, ending fittingly with one last obstacle for him to overcome. The Tide and the Texas Tech Red Raiders fought to a 10-10 tie with less than three minutes to play. Bama was more than 80 yards from the Tech goal when Croyle jogged onto the field. In the stands, his parents looked at each other and agreed that the setting was perfect. This was one more obstacle, and their son could overcome it.

In the huddle, Croyle simply said, "We're gonna get it done." They did, moving downfield with time running out. Jamie Christensen booted a 45-yard field goal on the final play. 13-10 Tide.

As an Alabama football team does in a game, we all face obstacles in life. They are those things that stand in the way of where we are and where we want to be or what we want to do. Some, such as physical problems, are not of our own making. Many of the barriers or roadblocks we face, however, are self-inflicted, a product of the poor choices we make.

We also face spiritual obstacles to our faith life. They keep us from getting where we want to be in our relationship with God. Unlike the privation and the suffering that Paul experienced, our spiritual obstacles are self-inflicted. They're the product of our sin or our indifference (itself a sin). Coldness seeps into our heart, and we allow a distance to grow between God and us, a distance that many of us have felt at one time or another.

What can we do? We remember that it wasn't God who put that obstacle in place; we must move, take action. We drop the sin and actively pursue that broken relationship. We turn back to God, open our hearts to him again, and kick that barrier down.

I had a little smirk on my face.
— Brodie Croyle, on taking the field to face his last obstacle at Alabama

**The only obstacles between God and us
are the ones we erect.**

NO APOLOGIES

Read Acts 4:1-21.

"For we cannot help speaking about what we have seen and heard" (v. 20).

Sophomore defensive tackle Bob Baumhower expected to get an apology from Bear Bryant for his mistakes. Yeah, right.

Baumhower was All-SEC as a senior in 1976 and a two-time second-team All-America. He went on to a Pro-Bowl NFL career.

All that was in front of him, though, when his freshman season started badly; the coaches put him on the offensive line. "I hated it," he said. "I wanted to play defense." In the spring, the coaches moved him back to the defensive line, and he emerged as the No. 2 defensive tackle.

Baumhower admitted that when he came back in the fall he was not in great shape. Still, he was astounded on the first day of practice when he was handed an orange jersey. That meant he was last string. After three days, he pushed the jersey basket back at the equipment manager and announced he was quitting.

Later that day, a teammate told Baumhower Bryant wanted to see his dad and him in his office. The proud player figured that the coach was going to apologize for his mistakes and reinstate him to the team. He was sadly mistaken.

Instead, Bryant handed the sophomore a list of the players ahead of him on the depth chart and told him what they had done to prepare for the season. "What did you do to get better?" he asked. "I don't think you're a quitter. I just think you're frustrated."

"At that moment, at that meeting" Baumhower said, "my whole outlook changed." He understood that Bryant saw his potential and was giving him an opportunity to play. "Everything I did later at Alabama [and in the pros] started at that meeting."

Including no longer expecting apologies from his head coach.

We usually apologize when we wrong or injure another person whether it's bumping someone with a shopping cart in the supermarket, causing an automobile accident, or being uncharacteristically harsh or cruel. Courtesy, forthrightness, our sense of justice, and our Christ-centered desire to repair the damage to a relationship demand apologies from us sometime.

But too many Christians in the increasingly hostile environment that is contemporary America find themselves apologizing for their faith and the temerity they display in inviting someone to church or saying the name of Jesus in their presence. We shouldn't. To apologize for our faith is to declare in effect that we are ashamed of Jesus.

Like Peter and John, we do not have to tell anyone we're sorry for our faith or abashedly try to excuse our actions in the name of Christ. We are Christians, heart and soul. And don't those who purposely flaunt their behavior in Christians' faces tell us, "If you don't like it, live with it"? We're just doing the same. Only in our case, we're talking about living eternally.

I figured [Bear Bryant] knew he had messed up and was going to ask me to come back to the team.
— *Bob Baumhower on expecting an apology from the Bear*

We should never apologize for Jesus.

DAY 28

LONELY TIMES

Read 1 Kings 19:1-10.

"I alone am left, and they are seeking my life, to take it away" (v. 10b).

Corky Simpson stood alone, vilified and ridiculed by his peers. What was his crime? He voted Alabama No. 1 in the country.

In 1992, Simpson was a longtime sportswriter for the *Tucson Citizen* in Arizona. In preparing for the college football season, he spoke with — among others — Bill Lumpkin of the *Birmingham Post-Herald,* Alabama Sports Information Director Larry White, and Crimson Tide head coach Gene Stallings. He took the trio quite seriously when they declared that Alabama had what it took to win the national championship in 1992.

Trusting their judgment, Simpson used his vote in the Associated Press weekly poll to list Alabama as the No. 1 team in the country. He was the only one.

Virtually every pundit in the country voted for Miami or Washington. Then there was that lone "loose cannon voting in the Associated Press weekly poll that year, one guy out of 62 who thought the Crimson Tide was #1 . . . all season long."

Simpson remained anonymous until a writer for the *Decatur Daily* in Decatur, Ala., "went to the trouble to find out who the nut was voting week after week for Alabama." The paper exposed him in an article and things turned ugly.

Not only did Simpson endure razzing from his fellow sportswriters, but he received a lot of "unhappy, even hateful mail." Sports talk shows from all over the country questioned his knowledge of the game, not to mention his sanity and his sobriety.

But during those lonely times, Simpson stuck to his guns. He never changed his ballot. And when the Sugar Bowl was over and Alabama had blasted the supposedly unbeatable Hurricanes, he — alone — was vindicated. Alabama was the national champion.

We all know loneliness even sometimes when we're standing in the midst of a crowd. Like love, fear, and despair, loneliness is an elemental part of "the human condition"; it's universal.

Every single one of us is alone in a sense because we can never completely bridge the gap between our consciousness and that of another person, even the ones we love the most. We can't really know another person; that person can't really know us. We are all strangers to each other.

There is one powerful exception, however: Almighty God. As Elijah found out in an unforgettable way, God is always with us, knowing exactly what we are experiencing, thinking, and feeling. God meets us in the deepest and darkest corners of our hearts and minds. Through the Holy Spirit, God is not just with us as other people are but is in us as other people can never be.

The heartwarming truth is that the person of faith is not alone and is never truly alone. God is with us always, even when we don't notice.

I never doubted that the Crimson Tide was the best team in the country.
— Corky Simpson on the 1992 national champions

Loneliness is part of being human — until we know God, and then we're never alone again.

DAY 29

UNCERTAIN TIMES

Read Psalm 18:1-6, 20-29.

"The Lord is my rock . . . in whom I take refuge. He is my shield, and the horn of my salvation, my stronghold" (v. 2).

Reggie Ragland was so uncertain that he wondered if he could even play football at a high level.

"SEC coaches fell over themselves chasing after" Ragland out of high school. Alabama got him. When he hit the Tide practice field for the first time in 2012, he was an impressive specimen. He "didn't look like a freshman, his legs as thick as tree trunks."

But this wasn't high school anymore; reality set in, and everything changed. He struggled with head coach Nick Saban's defensive system. Fellow linebackers Nico Johnson, C.J. Mosley, and Trey DePriest buried him on the depth chart. Classmates T.J. Yeldon, Amari Cooper, and Landon Collins became stars while he played little his freshman season and saw limited action as a backup in 2013. Eleven of his 17 tackles that sophomore season came on special teams.

Ragland just wasn't anything special anymore, and he began to believe it. He became uncertain about his talent, about whether he could really play big-time football. He wondered if he could ever regain the confidence he had had in high school.

His uncertainty remained as the 2014 season neared. Johnson and Mosley were gone, and a starting linebacker spot was being handed to him. Still . . .?

One day, Ragland turned to Collins and expressed his uncertainty out loud. "I've been out for years," he said. The All-SEC safety told him to just go out and play football. "You've been doing it for how many years?" he asked rhetorically. "All you have to do is go out there, play your game and just ball."

Ragland listened, regained his confidence, and found his footing. Saban said that as Ragland gained experience, he got better and better. He was All-SEC in 2014. As a senior in 2015, he was the SEC Defensive Player of the Year and a unanimous All-American.

Even when we believe that Alabama will field another great football team, we have some uncertainty because nothing in sport is a sure thing. If it were, it wouldn't be any fun.

Life is like that. We never know what's in store for us or what's going to happen next. We can be riding high one day with a job promotion, good health, a nice family, and sunny weather. Only a short time later, we can be unemployed, sick, divorced, and/or broke. When we place our trust in life itself and its rewards, we are certain to face uncertain times.

We must search out a haven, a place where we know we can find certainty to ease our trepidation and anxiety about life's uncertainties. We can find that haven, that rock, by dropping to our knees. There, we can find that certainty — every time.

Our life and times are uncertain. The Lord God Almighty is sure — and is only a prayer away.

Because I hadn't played in a couple of years, everything was fast.
— Reggie Ragland explaining his uncertainty

Only God offers certainty amid life's uncertainty.

DAY 30

HURRY UP & WAIT

Read Acts 1:1-14.

"Do not leave Jerusalem, but wait for the gift my Father promised, which you have heard me speak about" (v. 4).

For the Alabama softball team, the long wait finally ended.

On June 6, 2012, Alabama met Oklahoma in the deciding game of the best-of-three finals of the Women's College World Series. It was Alabama's eighth appearance in the CWS, the first coming in 2000. The best finish had been third, three times.

Yet, here they were, only one win away from putting an end to the long wait for a national championship. As writer Graham Hays put it, "The Crimson Tide didn't want to wait any longer. They just wanted to play."

But they had to wait some more. A steady rain forced a three-hour delay in the start of the game. When it finally did begin, the Sooners slammed a pair of home runs to take a 3-0 lead and all the momentum. Meanwhile, Alabama "looked helpless" against Oklahoma's pitcher, the national player of the year.

The Tide's title hopes may have been rescued by — of all things — another wait. Kaila Hunt singled to start the fourth, but the next two batters made outs. By this time, it was raining again, and OU's star pitcher lost her grip on the ball. She tossed a walk and three wild pitches. That made it 3-1. Oklahoma's coach visited the umpires and asked for a weather delay. She got it.

Patrick Murphy protested to no avail. Good thing. OU's team

sat in the dugout while Alabama's players basically threw a party. They gathered in front of the dugout in the rain and exchanged cheers with their fans. They kept getting louder and louder. "With each passing minute, it felt more and more like something had shifted." It had: all the momentum.

After a 13-minute delay, the Tide scored three more times in the fourth and eventually won 5-4. The long, long wait was over.

You rush to your doctor's appointment and wind up sitting in the appropriately named waiting room for an hour. You wait in the concessions line at an Alabama game. You're put on hold when you call a tragically misnamed "customer service" center. All of that waiting is time in which we seem to do nothing but feel the precious minutes of our life ticking away.

Sometimes we even wait for God. We have needs, and in our desperation, we call upon the Lord. We are then disappointed if we don't get an immediate answer to our prayers.

But Jesus' last command to his disciples was to wait. Moreover, the entire of our Christian life is spent in an attitude of waiting for Jesus' return. While we wait for God, we hold steadfast to his promises, and we continue our ministry; we remain in communion with him through prayer and devotion.

In other words, we don't just wait; we grow stronger in our faith. Waiting for God is never time lost.

Alabama waited a long time to hold a trophy in Oklahoma City.
— *ESPN's Graham Hays*

**Since God acts on his time and not ours,
we often must wait for him,
using the time to strengthen our faith.**

DAY 31

FUSSBUDGETS

Read Philippians 2:12-18.

"Do everything without complaining or arguing, so that you may become blameless and pure" (vv. 14, 15a).

It seemed everybody was fussing and complaining. You would have thought the Tide's season was in the toilet.

Four games into the 1994 football season, few folks seemed very happy with Alabama's team. "Our offense is not close to where it needs to be," declared offensive coordinator Homer Smith. "We need to be a lot better than we are," grumbled defensive coordinator Bill Oliver. Head coach Gene Stallings called the team's offense pathetic and said the defense looked adequate because "we haven't played anybody who was real good on offense."

Outside the athletic department, fans were grousing. Radio shows were "on fire with terrible Tide talk." Paul Finebaum, he years later of the *SEC Network*, noted that Stallings had been talking a lot about his Texas ranch. Said the Birmingham radio talk-show host, "There's a lot of feeling he may be spending a lot of time back at his ranch soon."

The Tide's season obviously was a total disaster at this point. Well, not exactly, In fact, the team was 4-0. It was truly, though, "the most unsatisfying 4-0 in the land, a perfect record laden with disdain and suspicion." The squad had thumped 1-AA's Tennessee-Chattanooga, topped perennial doormat Vanderbilt 17-7, slipped by a bad Arkansas team 13-6, and beaten "routinely unimpressive" Tulane 20-10. Alabama was dead last in the SEC in passing. As writer Douglass S. Looney put it, "Winning ugly is not inspiring to watch, and it has been making everybody cranky."

Then came the Georgia game of Oct. 1. Jay Barker threw for 396 yards, and Alabama rallied in the last quarter to stun the Bulldogs 29-28. A lot of that complaining suddenly stopped.

The team went on to finish 12-1, losing only to Florida by one point in the SEC title game.

Our usual and immediate reaction when we are wronged or are unhappy about something is to complain. Fussing may be natural, but it isn't spiritual.

Paul urged us to stifle our complaints, which demonstrates the depth of our faith. Well now, just how does that work? Complaining is brought on by our circumstances; it's aimed at something or somebody. But when we complain, we are in fact declaring our failure to perceive that God is in charge of the moment. To grumble and to whine is thus to take our eyes off God. Complaining is nothing more than a spiritually immature reaction to a temporarily bothersome situation.

The more faith-filled response to a situation that tempts us to complain is prayer. While praying may not immediately resolve whatever it is that has driven our blood pressure up, it nevertheless allows us to escape from the unpleasantness blameless before God. And that's never anything to complain about.

For some reason, I've gotten awful stupid lately.
  — Gene Stallings reacting to the complaining and criticism in 2004

**Complaining is an unspiritual response to a
temporary situation better resolved by prayer.**

BROKEN DREAMS

Read Joel 2:28-32.

"I will pour out my Spirit on all people. . . . Your old men will dream dreams" (v. 28).

Because one of Roger Shultz's dreams was shattered, another came true that he never imagined would.

As a youngster, Shultz dreamed of being a running back. He was a big guy, but in his mind he was blessed with deceptive speed. His plan was simple: Give him the ball and get out of the way. His dream came true for one season.

Shultz always played on the line in youth leagues. His family moved while he was in junior high, and his new coach asked him where he played. Shultz didn't hesitate. "Running back," he said. Running back it was, all 6-foot-2, 269 lbs. of him.

"I couldn't cut, I couldn't see openings downfield, and I definitely didn't have breakaway speed," Shultz recalled. The only time he remembered breaking a tackle was when he went head-on against a "little bitty safety." "I think the longest touchdown run I had was about six inches," he said.

When the family moved again, Shultz's dream of running the ball ended. He wound up at right guard and stayed there through high school, starting for three seasons.

Eventually, the colleges came calling. Bama head coach Ray Perkins contacted him one day and got right to the point. "We'd like to offer you a scholarship," he said.

And so another Shultz dream came true. He grew up a Tide fan and had always dreamed of playing in Tuscaloosa. "I never thought that would be a possibility," he said. His answer to Perkins? "I'll take it. . . . I'm committing right now. . . . I want you to put it in the papers. I want everyone to know."

He was deep in the depth chart his freshman season of 1986. When injuries decimated the centers early in 1987, he had a one-day tryout. The next day he was No. 1 on the depth chart, and he started on Saturday. He wound up a four-year starter at center, was a freshman All-America, and was All-SEC in 1989 and 1990.

Like Roger Shultz, we all have particular dreams. Perhaps to make a million dollars, write the Great American Novel or find the perfect spouse. More likely than not, though, we gradually lose our hold on those dreams. They slip away from us as we surrender them to the reality of everyday living.

But we also have general dreams. For world peace. For an end to hunger. That no child should ever again be afraid. These dreams we hold doggedly onto as if something inside us tells us that even though the world gets itself into a bigger mess every year, one day everything will be all right.

That's because it will be. God has promised a time when his spirit will rule the world. Jesus spoke of a time when he will return to claim his kingdom. In that day, our dreams of peace and plenty and the banishment of hate and want will be reality.

Our dreams based on God's promises will come true.

I didn't think I was good enough to play at Alabama.
— Roger Shultz on a dream that he thought would never happen

Dreams based on God's promises will come true.

DAY 33

RISK TAKERS

Read Esther 4:1-14; 5:1-8.

"Any man or woman who approaches the king without being summoned [will] be put to death" (v. 4:11a).

Damion Square could have played college football just about anywhere. When he committed, though, he took a risk. That's because he opted for Alabama.

Square was a heralded recruit from Texas. A number of programs that were on the top of their game recruited him hard. And then there was Alabama.

This was 2008, and when Tide coaches bragged about their twelve national championships, Square was not impressed. "In my mind," he said, "I'm thinking that the last one was in 1992. That's a long time." Most recently, Alabama was 33-30 over the last five seasons with not a single appearance in a BCS bowl.

But Square bought into the Alabama mystique and the high expectations and dedication of second-year Tide head coach Nick Saban and his staff. He was a part of one of the most heralded signing classes in Alabama history. Among others, it included Mark Ingram, Julio Jones, Barrett Jones, and Dont'a Hightower.

At first, it seemed he had made a mistake. Square was red-shirted in 2008 and then missed most of the 2009 season with injuries. But everything changed in 2010 when he moved into the starting lineup for good. He wound up starting 33 games at Alabama, including all 13 in 2011 and all 14 in 2012.

In a five-year span, Square and his teammates made college football history by winning 61 games. They also won three national titles and two SEC championships.

After his career ended with the win over Notre Dame in the BCS title game of Jan. 7, 2013, Square called his time at Alabama "something special." He declared he could not have had a better college experience. The risk he took turned out to be worth it.

Life's risks come in all shapes and sizes. Asking someone for a date, starting a business or a new job, crossing a street — they're all risks. Inherent in any risk is a choice, conscious or not. We choose after weighing the possible gain against the possible loss.

That holds true in our faith life. God has a plan for our lives; each of us is born with a divine purpose. Satan's paltry, unimaginative plan is to thwart God's plan. Thus, when we live according to our own desires, we are deciding that chasing our own goals is worth the risk of rejecting God's plan.

Following God's plan is risky, all right. Just look at Esther. Or Jesus. It's risky because it involves surrender; we don't know what God will call us to do for him. As always, the question is the same: Is the possible gain in following God worth the possible loss?

The answer is a resounding yes. It's not just that we receive a life far beyond the ordinary, one that involves purpose, joy, love, excitement, and fulfillment. It's that we receive eternal life with God. That alone is worth any risk

[Damion Square] came when the program wasn't as good, and that's a great commitment.
— Tide defensive coordinator Kirby Smart on the risk Square took

Following God is risky; it's worth it.

DAY 34

GOOD ADVICE

Read Isaiah 9:2-7.

"And he will be called Wonderful Counselor" (v. 9:6b).

Dana Duckworth consistently followed her mother's advice; Alabama reaped the benefits.

On July 15, 2014, Duckworth was named the first new head coach of the Alabama women's gymnastics team in 36 years. That first year marked her 20th season as part of the program. Yet, without her mother's advice, she may well have never been involved with either gymnastics or Alabama.

For decades, Duckworth's mother was a prominent coach and judge in the gymnastics community. "I literally grew up in the gym," Duckworth said. She was competing in gymnastics by the time she was 7 years old. "I did it because it was fun," she said.

When she was 13, she started work on a complicated move as part of her floor exercise. She couldn't hit it. She either landed on her head or botched the landing. She hurt herself so often that she grew afraid of the move and so frustrated that she decided to quit.

Her mother didn't mandate or force but stepped in with some advice. "You can do all these other things," she said, "and you're going to let one skill" drive you to quit? "Let's do everything but that skill and see if you still love gymnastics." Duckworth did and she did. She soon performed the skill and forgot about quitting.

Duckworth became one of the most highly recruited gymnasts in the country. She narrowed the list to five, loved the first school she visited, and told her mom that was the place.

Again, her mother proffered advice. "You have four more visits committed and plane tickets," she said. "You need to work the process." So Duckworth followed her mother's advice and made the second visit on her list — to Alabama.

Like Dana Duckworth, we all need a little advice now and then. More often than not, we turn to professional counselors, who are all over the place. Marriage counselors, grief counselors, guidance counselors in our schools, rehabilitation counselors, all sorts of mental health and addiction counselors — We even have pet counselors. No matter what our situation or problem, we can find plenty of advice for the taking.

The problem, of course, is that we find advice easy to offer but hard to take. We also have a rueful tendency to solicit the wrong source for advice, seeking counsel that doesn't really solve our problem but that instead enables us to continue with it.

Our need for outside advice, for an independent perspective on our situation, is actually God-given. God serves many functions in our lives, but one role clearly delineated in his Word is that of Counselor. Jesus himself is described as the "Wonderful Counselor." All the advice we need in our lives is right there for the asking; we don't even have to pay for it except with our faith. God is always there for us: to listen, to lead, and to guide.

'Mom, I want to go there.' 'Dana, you have more visits.'
— Dana Duckworth and her mom's advice during recruiting

**We all need and seek advice in our lives,
but the ultimate and most wonderful Counselor
is of divine and not human origin.**

DAY 35

THE GOOD FIGHT

Read 2 Corinthians 10:1-6.

"For though we live in the world, we do not wage war as the world does. The weapons we fight with are not the weapons of the world" (vv. 3-4a).

Cyrus Kouandjio was a born fighter; he inherited it.

Kouandjio was a two-year starter at left tackle (2012, '13) for the Tide. He was first-team All-SEC in 2013. His older brother, Arie, teamed with Cyrus at left guard to make up one side of the Tide's offensive line in 2013.

Cyrus once said that the mentality that let him fight to succeed came from his dad. His father was a child in Cameroon when civil war came to his village. With his 2-year-old sister on his back, he fled to the forest and hid out for years. Somehow, he survived.

When Cyrus was 4, the Kouandjio family came to America. Dad spent the last of his money to enroll his children in a private school. Those were not good times for Cyrus. He often sat in the school cafeteria with nothing to eat. To get home, he'd take old bus passes and paste them together to look official. The drivers knew but let him on anyway. Once after football practice, he had no way of getting home, so he walked, wearing his football gear.

How did he make it through, where did he find the motivation at such a young age? Cyrus knew. "It's like a mentality," he said. "It was innate." From his father, he inherited that determination to fight, to survive, and to succeed no matter what.

Cyrus opted for the NFL draft in 2014. He reflected that "the promise of a future free of financial concerns [was] almost too much to fathom." To him, the money was more than just riches because it gave him the chance to help his father out.

He was drafted in the second round and signed a 4-year contract for $4.8 million, including a $1.8 million signing bonus.

Just as the Kouandjio family fought to survive and succeed, shouldn't Christians fight for their Lord? Following Jesus' admonition to turn the other cheek has rendered many a Christian meek and mild in the name of obedience. But we would do well to remember that the Lord we follow once bullwhipped a bunch of folks who had turned God's temple into a flea market.

With Christianity in America under attack as never before, we must stand up for and fight for our faith. Who else is there to stand up for Jesus if not you? Our pretty little planet — including our nation — is a battleground between good and evil. We are far from helpless in this fight because God has provided us with a powerful set of weapons. Prayer, faith, hope, love, the Word of God itself and the Holy Spirit — these are the weapons at our command with which to vanquish evil and godlessness.

We are called by God to use them, to fight the good fight, not just in our own lives but in our nation and in our world.

What me and my brother went through was a mentality that this is who you are and you've always been a fighter. It's almost in your blood.
— Cyrus Kouandjio

**'Stand Up, Stand Up for Jesus' is not
an antiquated hymn but a contemporary call
to battle for our Lord.**

DEMOLITION MEN

Read Genesis 7.

"Every living thing on the face of the earth was wiped out" (v. 23a).

The Vols had rallied to tie the game and had all the momentum. Then in the space of five minutes, the Tide demolished them.

On Oct. 20, 1973, the 5-0 Tide hosted the 5-0 Tennessee Volunteers in Birmingham. In public the week of the game, Bear Bryant ridiculed the 14-point favorites Las Vegas bookies had made his second-ranked team. In private, he knew better. After all, he had already bought a mess of cigars to light up after the win.

Sure enough, the Tide jumped out to that 14-point lead at 21-7. By the fourth quarter, though, Tennessee had fought back to knot the score at 21. Then came the demolition.

Behind "a wedge of Redshirt blockers who ricocheted off one another like tenpins in their eagerness to cooperate," Robin Cary returned a Tennessee punt 64 yards for a touchdown. Wilbur Jackson took a simple sweep and turned it into an 80-yard touchdown romp. Rattled, the Vols fumbled and Bama scored.

Three touchdowns in five minutes, seven seconds. 42-21. Demolition complete.

Bryant was so impressed with his team that in the dressing room after the game, having dispensed a prayer and the cigars, he mounted a bench, waved the bedlam to silence, and declared, "You're the greatest bunch I've ever been around." Then as if to realize he might be perceived as disparaging some of his other teams, he added, "Either that or the greatest bunch of con men."

But this *was* one of the Bear's greatest teams. They rolled to an 11-0 season, demolishing their opponents. Nobody came closer to them than 14 points. Only a 1-point loss to Notre Dame in one of the greatest bowl games of all time cost them the national title.

We've heard a lot across recent decades about "weapons of mass destruction." The phrase conjures up frightening images of entire cities and countries being laid to waste. The population is annihilated; buildings are flattened; the infrastructure is destroyed; air and water are polluted; foodstuff is rendered inedible.

While the hideous weapons we have so zealously created can indeed wreak destruction, nothing we have can equal the weapon of mass destruction that is the wrath of God. Only once has its full fury been loosed upon his creation; the result was the mass destruction unleashed by the flood.

God has promised that he will never again destroy everything with water. When Christ returns, though, mass destruction of a particular kind will again lay waste the Earth.

Until then, as part of the ongoing battle between good and evil, we have the ultimate weapon of mass destruction at our disposal; it is our faith. With it, we play a vital part in what will be God's ultimate mass destruction: The total eradication of evil in the Day of our Lord.

It was a five-minute burst of deadly reckoning.
— *Writer John Underwood on Bama's demolition of Tennessee in 1973*

**Our faith is a weapon of mass destruction,
playing a key role in the eradication of evil.**

GOLDEN SILENCE

Read Psalm 46.

"Be still, and know that I am God" (v. 10a).

Mark Barron is literally the strong, silent type.

Barron was a two-time All-American Crimson Tide strong safety in 2010 and 2011 and a three-time All-SEC player. He was taken in the first round of the 2012 NFL draft.

In this age when "waxing on about the subject of the self is all too frequently part of a college star's approach," Barron was an exception while he was in Tuscaloosa. Writer Andrew Lawrence said Barron took "to campus life like a Trappist monk, meting out words almost reluctantly." In other words, Mark Barron never talked too much.

To Tide fans, only a few of whom had ever heard his voice, he thus became "an enigma wrapped in a body that's been NFL-ready since high school." Barron stood 6'2" tall and weighed in at 218 lbs. He also sprinted the 40-yard dash in less than 4.5 seconds, "about half as long as it takes him to express an opinion." While he was playing for the Tide, Barron didn't tweet and granted interviews about as rarely as he was beaten on the field — which was virtually never.

When Barron reluctantly held a news conference to announce his decision to return for his senior season (2011), the affair lasted 80 seconds. That's how long it took for him to read a statement.

"My leadership style is more my example," he once said in a

flurry of words. A demure high five was about as self-indulgent and as animated as he ever got during a game. Calling the signals for the secondary, he always ran over to tell his teammates directly instead of barking out his orders across the field.

For Mark Barron at Alabama, silence was truly golden. He let his play on the field do his talking for him.

Spiritual disciplines are the tools we have at our disposal to develop our faith life, the means that we employ to consciously draw closer to God, to deepen that relationship. For the individual Christian, these include prayer, the study of Scripture, fasting, and meditation or silence in the presence of God.

It's difficult to imagine a committed follower of Jesus Christ not praying or reading and studying Scripture on a regular basis, preferably daily. But the practice of silence should also be integrated into our daily disciplines. (Fasting is a matter for another day.) In fact, a period of silence before God is so interconnected with praying and Scripture study that the three disciplines can actually make up one intertwined devotional time.

Prayer for many Christians is one-sided: We talk, we expect God to listen. It's like sending an e-mail and then blocking the address to prevent a reply. Time spent in silence — meditating on God without distraction or interruption — gives God a chance to enter into the conversation.

Whose voice is the more important one here: yours or God's?

I'll say things when I have to.

— Mark Barron

**How in the world can we hear God's voice
if we don't shut up and listen?**

DAY 38

LOVE OF YOUR LIFE

Read 1 John 4:7-21.

"Whoever does not love does not know God, because God is love" (v. 8).

Mal Moore was a fortunate man in that he had not one, but two great loves in his life.

The most public one, of course, was the University of Alabama. He was a quarterback for Bear Bryant and a coach for Alabama for 22 seasons. He was the only offensive coordinator Bryant ever named and was instrumental in the installation of the legendary wishbone offense prior to the 1971 season. When newly hired head coach Ray Perkins fired Moore and other offensive assistants in 1982, he broke down and cried. He returned to Tuscaloosa in 1990 as Gene Stallings' offensive coordinator.

But there was a less public, more private love in Mal Moore's life. That was his wife, Charlotte. In 1968, in his fourth year as an Alabama assistant, the two married. Some twenty-five happy years followed.

Things changed, however, in 1993. As the season moved along, Moore's hectic schedule was frequently interrupted by calls to come home. Soon the calls came almost hourly. During the 1993 Gator Bowl trip, other coaches' wives quietly told Moore what he already knew: Something was amiss with Charlotte.

She was diagnosed with Alzheimer's, forcing Moore to choose between the two loves of his life. He chose Charlotte, giving up coaching to become an associate athletic director, which gave him more time for her. Five years later, he was promoted to athletic director and carried out one of the most successful tenures in college sports history. Charlotte died in 2010; he died in 2013.

Moore is the only person in history to earn ten national title rings in football. Perhaps it was the eleventh ring — the one Charlotte gave him — that meant the most of all to him.

Your heart rate accelerates, your blood pressure jumps, your mouth runs dry, your vision blurs, and you start stammering. Either you've got the flu or the one you're in love with just walked into the room and smiled at you. Fortunately, if the attraction is based on more than hormones and eye candy, the feverish frenzy that characterizes newfound love matures into a deeper, more meaningful affection. If it didn't, we'd probably die from exhaustion, stroke, heart failure, or a combination thereof.

We pursue true love with a desperation and a ferocity that is unmatched by any other desire. Ultimately, the Christian life is about that same search, about falling in love and becoming a partner in a deep-seated, satisfying, ever-growing and ever-deepening relationship. The Christian life is about loving so fiercely and so completely that love is not something we're in but something we are. The object of our love is the greatest and most faithful lover of them all: God.

I cannot put into words what this institution that I have been a part of for over 50 years means to me.
— Mal Moore at his retirement declaring his love for Alabama

God is head-over-heels in love with you;
like any lover, he wants you to return the love.

DAY 39

OLD-FASHIONED

Read Leviticus 18:1-5.

"You must obey my laws and be careful to follow my decrees. I am the Lord your God" (v. 4).

Blast from the past, old-fashioned football. So it was when the Hogs from Arkansas came to Tuscaloosa in 2013.

Alabama had become quite accustomed to going up against all those newfangled offenses that the likes of Texas A&M and Ole Miss threw at its defense. The defensive coaches were used to scheming for those new designs "that spread the field and push the tempo like a young driver blowing through traffic stops."

So along came Arkansas, and for one afternoon, the Crimson Tide defense found itself back in the 1980s. Or thereabouts.

In December 2012, Bret Bielema took the head Hawg job. He brought with him the "old-fashioned" physical style of offense that had been his hallmark through his six successful seasons at Wisconsin.

Bielema built his offense on a power running game, which in college football in 2013 had pretty much "gone the way of the Dodo." Arkansas lined up in the I-formation and ran the ball — usually right at anyone they could find.

As it turned out, that old-fashioned formation was brand new to the Tide's defensive players, who had been raised on dual-threat quarterbacks and hurry-up-no-huddle offenses. Safety Vinnie Sunseri's immediate reaction was a smirk when someone asked him the last time he had seen such an offense. "It will be a little bit different," he eventually said, "because we have played those spread teams that like to sling it around a little bit."

The Hawgs didn't "sling it around a little bit" when they met Alabama on Oct. 19. They didn't do much of anything as the Tide coasted 52-0. "We pride ourselves on being a tough, relentless defense," said cornerback Deion Belue. On this day, old-fashioned defense bested old-fashioned offense.

Usually, when we refer to some person, some idea, or some institution as old-fashioned, we deliver a full-fledged or at least thinly veiled insult. They're out of step with the times and the mores, hopelessly out of date, totally irrelevant, and quite useless.

For the people of God, however, "old-fashioned" is exactly the lifestyle we should pursue. The throwbacks are the ones who value honor, dignity, sacrifice, and steadfastness, who can be counted on to tell the truth and to do what they say. Old-fashioned folks shape their lives according to eternal values and truths, the ones handed down by almighty God.

These ancient laws and decrees are still relevant to contemporary life because they direct us to a lifestyle of holiness and righteousness that serves us well every single day. Such a way of living allows us to escape the ultimately hopeless life to which so many have doomed themselves in the name of being modern.

There's comfort in the familiar returning from extinction.
— Writer Alex Scarborough on Arkansas' old-fashioned offense

The ancient lifestyle God calls us to still leads us to a life of contentment, peace, and joy, which never grows old-fashioned.

DAY 40

TURNAROUND

Read Acts 9:1-22.

*"All those who heard him were astonished and asked,
'Isn't he the man who raised havoc in Jerusalem among
those who call on this name?'" (v. 21)*

Bear Bryant believed Southern Cal was beaten, over and done
with. Then the game turned around.

Alabama and USC met on Oct. 8, 1977, in the Los Angeles Coli-
seum. The Tide was on its way to an 11-1 season; the Trojans had
won 15 straight and were ranked No. 1.

As writer Joe Jares put it, given the school's proximity to Hollywood and USC's penchant for last-minute wins, "the assumption
may be made that football game plans are prepared by the
school's cinema department, not the coaching staff." Right until
the last few seconds, this looked like another one of those days.

Trailing 3-0, the Tide drove 51 yards in the third quarter with
fullback Johnny Davis scoring from the 2. USC answered with a
second field goal after the Tide defense held at the 1-inch line.

Another Bama drive resulted in a touchdown from halfback
Tony Nathan. Less than a minute later, nose guard Curtis McGriff
tipped a pass to sophomore defensive end Wayne Hamilton. He
returned his theft to the Trojan 8, and Nathan took it from there.

It was 21-6 and the Bear later admitted that he thought USC
was "completely beaten."

But the game suddenly turned around. The Trojans drove 91

yards for a score, forced a punt, and then moved 79 yards for a touchdown with 35 seconds left to play. Trailing by 1, they went for two and the win. Hamilton again came through, getting to the Trojan quarterback and forcing a feeble toss that was intercepted.

The game had turned around, but not quite enough to suit the Trojans. Alabama came away with a 21-20 win.

Like football teams do during a game, we often look for some way to turn our lives around. Oh, we may not be headed to prison, be bankrupt, or be plagued by an addiction. Maybe we can't find a purpose to our life and are just drifting.

Still, our situation often seems untenable to us. Thus, we sink into gloom and despair, wasting our time, our emotions, and our energy by fretting about how bad things are and how they will never get better. How in the world can we turn things around?

Turn to Jesus; as the old hymn urges, trust and obey him. If it's that simple, then why hesitate? Well, it's also that complicated as Paul discovered when he experienced one of the most dramatic turnarounds in history. To surrender to Jesus is to wind up with a new life and to wind up with a new life, we have to surrender to Jesus. We have to give up control.

What's to lose? After all, if we're looking for a way to turn our lives around, we're not doing such a good job of running things. What's to gain? Life worth living, both temporal and eternal.

I have never seen a team that I thought was completely beaten, then in the fourth quarter come back so strong.
— Bear Bryant on USC's turnaround in the 1977 game

**A life in need of turning around
needs Jesus at the wheel.**

DAY 41

NICE GUY

Read Proverbs 3:1-12.

"Let love and faithfulness never leave you; . . . Then you will win favor and a good name in the sight of God and man" (vv. 3a, 4).

Considering the extreme passions that surround the Iron Bowl rivalry, what Blake Sims did for a fellow college student was downright unbelievably nice.

In his one season as Bama's starting quarterback (2014), Sims threw for 3,487 yards, a school single-season passing record. He was Second-Team All-SEC. On Sept. 20, in only his fourth start, Sims led the Tide to a 42-21 beatdown of the Florida Gators by throwing for 445 yards, the second most in school history behind Scott Hunter's 484 yards in 1969.

But as one writer put it, "That wasn't the most significant thing Sims did — not even close."

The Alabama senior played the game wearing a purple bracelet on his right wrist. It read "Kayla" and "Joshua 1:7." The Bible verse says, "Be strong and very courageous." For athletes to wear scripture on their bodies or uniforms during a game isn't that unusual. But what about "Kayla"? Now that was really different.

"Kayla" was 19-year-old Kayla Perry, who was battling a vicious form of cancer. When Sims wore her name into the showdown with the Gators, she was an Auburn student.

Perry started a Facebook page to help raise awareness of pediatric cancer research. Sims saw the page and wore the bracelet to support her efforts. After the game, Perry posted a reply that read in part, "Hey, guys, you know I'm an Auburn Tiger, but even college rivalries can come together when it matters."

Perry admitted that against the Gators, she really pulled hard for Sims to do well. On that day, he wasn't a rival; he was a nice guy who was a friend.

Former baseball manager Leo Durocher once declared, "Nice guys finish last." It's catchy and pithy, one of those memorable sports quotes that never seems to die. But it's wrong. Just look at Blake Sims; as Kayla Perry can tell you, he's a nice guy. Just ask the players on the other thirteen SEC football teams where nice guys finish after Sims quarterbacked the Tide to the 2014 SEC title.

Nice guys and gals as Scripture defines them always finish first in the only contest that matters: the one to secure God's favor. Proverbs tells us that God prefers people who live by his word, who show love to others, who trust in the Lord, who shun evil and thus do right, who tithe, and who do not resent the discipline required to live a faithful, godly life. The model for that life is Jesus Christ.

Good people, nice people who live as Jesus would have them do, never finish in second place, let alone last place. They are life's true champions. Their prize is the greatest trophy of all: Heaven.

We're really glad and thankful that he did that.
— *Kayla Perry on Blake Sims' bracelet*

**Nice people who follow Jesus finish in first place,
roaming around Heaven with God forever.**

DAY 42

CHEERS!

Read Matthew 21:1-11.

*"The crowds that went ahead of him and those that
followed shouted" (v. 9).*

As Jackie Traina rounded third and headed for home, among
those cheering the loudest for her was the Alabama legend whose
place she had taken in the game.

Traina is one of Alabama's greatest players, a four-time All-
America from 2011-14 and the SEC's Pitcher of the Year as a senior.

It was the senior Kelsi Dunne whom the freshman Traina
replaced on the mound on May 27, 2011, in the third and final
game of the super regional in Tuscaloosa. Dunne, a four-time
All-America and two-time SEC Pitcher of the Year who holds the
Tide career record for strikeouts, started the game. She had also
started the two earlier games and had thrown a 5-inning shutout
in game two after Stanford won the opener of the series.

Pitching her second game of the day in the withering Alabama
heat, Dunne was clearly tiring in the fourth inning. With one
out, head coach Patrick Murphy decided to take his ace out of the
biggest game of the year. He went to the bullpen and Traina, a
freshman. She got two ground balls and two outs on six pitches.

She kept throwing zeroes, but so did Stanford's pitcher. Then
in the bottom of the sixth, Traina popped a single. With two outs,
junior Cassie Reilly-Boccia drove a ball down the first-base line.
Traina took off and never stopped running.

When she made the turn at third, Murphy waved her home. He briefly joined her on the sprint. "Let's run together and hope one of us is safe," he later joked about what he was thinking. In the dugout, Dunne joined the voices cheering Traina home. "I was just like, 'Jackie, come, come, come!'" she said. "It was so exciting." Traina scored and pitched the seventh inning for the 1-0 win. The Tide was on its way to the Women's College World Series.

Chances are you go to work every day, do your job well, and then go home to your family. This country couldn't run without you; you're indispensable to the nation's efficiency. Even so, nobody cheers for you as they do for athletes like Kelsi Dunne and Jackie Traina. Your name probably will never elicit a standing ovation when a PA announcer calls it.

It's just as well, since public opinion is notoriously fickle. Consider what happened to Jesus. When he entered Jerusalem, he was the object of raucous cheering and an impromptu parade. The crowd's adulation reached such a frenzy they tore branches off trees and threw their clothes on the ground.

Five days later the crowd shouted again, only this time they screamed for Jesus' execution.

So don't worry too much about not having your personal set of cheering fans. Remember that you do have one personal cheerleader who will never stop pulling for you: God.

[Jackie] Traina scored the run of her life, with [Kelsi] Dunne one of the thousands of voices roaring their approval.
— *ESPN's Graham Hays*

**Just like the sports stars,
you do have a personal cheerleader: God.**

DAY 43

PRACTICE SESSION

Read 2 Peter 1:3-11.

"For if you do these things, you will never fail, and you will receive a rich welcome into the eternal kingdom of our Lord and Savior Jesus Christ" (vv. 10b-11).

T he practice just wouldn't end.

Wallace Wade is an Alabama and college football legend. He was the Tide's head coach from 1923-30, winning the school's first three national titles and compiling a 61-13-3 record.

Wade always put the football team before everything else. Fred Sington, a two-time All-America who was elected to the College Football Hall of Fame in 1955, (See Devotion No. 11.) found out just how dedicated Wade was. He pitched a no-hitter for the Tide baseball team and expected his coach to be proud of him. Instead, Wade chewed him out, asking him where he had been the day before when he was supposed to be running the hurdles and getting ready for football. "It showed me that Coach Wade was sort of sincere about football," Sington said.

Not surprisingly, Wade's practices "were tough, deliberate, painstakingly precise, and long." One practice, though, was a bit longer than most. The team was hard at it when Wade was told he had a phone call. He left to take it and practice went on.

Well, he didn't come back — and he didn't come back. No one knew the reason; maybe the phone call really was so important or maybe Wade was just testing his team. "He just left 'em out on the field," said Dave Sington, Fred's son, and an Alabama player in the 1950s. "Nobody would stop," Dave recalled his dad telling him. "They just kept on going."

Finally, after about two hours, a desperate team manager went in search of the truant head coach, found him, and asked him if the team could quit practicing. It could.

Imagine a football team that never practices, certainly a difficult endeavor in Wallace Wade's case. Or a play cast that doesn't rehearse. A preacher who never prepares, reviews, or practices his sermon beforehand. When the showdown comes, they would be revealed as inept bumblers that merit our disdain.

We practice something so that we will become good at it, so that it becomes so natural that we can pull it off without even having to think about it. Interestingly, if we are to live as Christ wants us to, then we must practice that lifestyle — and showing up at church and sitting stoically on a pew once a week does not constitute practice. To practice successfully, we must participate; we must do repeatedly whatever it is we want to be good at.

We must practice being like Christ by living like Christ every day of our lives. For Christians, practice is a lifestyle that doesn't make perfect — only Christ is perfect — but it does prepare us for the real thing: the day we meet God face to face and inherit Christ's kingdom.

I guess they were just scared to death of him.
— Dave Sington on why the Tide kept on practicing in Wade's absence

Practicing the Christian lifestyle doesn't make us perfect, but it does secure us a permanent place beside the perfect one.

DAY 44

LAUGH IT UP

Read Genesis 21:1-7.

"Sarah said, 'God has brought me laughter, and everyone who hears about this will laugh with me'" (v. 6).

Nick Saban actually had the reporters laughing. That was a hint that Alabama's game had really been different.

The Alabama-Texas A&M game of Sept. 14, 2013, was described as an "epic showdown": the top-ranked Tide against the sixth-ranked Aggies and Johnny Manziel in College Station. The teams gave everyone their money's worth, treating college football fans to one of the wildest and most exciting games ever.

When the contest was finally and exhaustingly over, the Crimson Tide had escaped with a 49-42 win. As *ESPN*'s Alex Scarborough put it, the game was "a shock to the senses in that it was so unlike everything we've come to expect from Alabama."

So how was this game so different that Saban could only laugh about it and pull the reporters along with him? A&M rolled up 626 yards, the most allowed by an Alabama defense in the history of the program. The Tide survived because A.J. McCarron and his offensive cohorts bailed the team out. McCarron threw for 334 yards, T.J. Yeldon rushed for 149 yards, and the Tide offense rolled up 568 yards of its own. "Old-school Alabama turned to new-school tactics, . . . showing a plucky, creative and even entertaining side never seen before."

After this game that turned perceptions of the Tide upside

down, Alabama's players tweeted how good Manziel and wide receiver Mike Evans were and the usually dour Saban smiled and laughed on camera.

The Tide head coach even cracked a joke, telling the reporters they had tried to make the game about a "61-year-old guy against that good quarterback." If that's the way it was, he said, "We didn't have much of a chance." The room broke into laughter.

Nick Saban will never be confused with a stand-up comedian. They're successful because they find humor in the world, and it's often hard for us to do that. "Laughter is foolish," an acerbic Solomon wrote in Ecclesiastes 2:2, his angst overwhelming him because he couldn't find much if anything in his world to laugh at.

We know how he felt. When we take a good look around at this world we live in, can we really find much to laugh at? It seems everywhere we look we find not just godlessness but ongoing and pervasive tragedy and misery.

Well, we can recognize as Sarah did that in God's innumerable gifts lie irresistible laughter. The great gift of Jesus provides us with more than enough reason to laugh no matter our situation. Through God's grace in Jesus Christ, we can laugh at death, at Satan, at the very gates of hell, at the world's pain.

Because they are of this world, our tears will pass. Because it is of God, our laughter will remain — forever.

You took ten years off my life.
— Nick Saban, meeting A&M's Kevin Sumlin at midfield in 2013 and
making a joke

Of the world, sorrow is temporary;
of God, laughter is forever.

THE GOOD STEWARDS

Read Luke 19:11-26.

"'[T]o everyone who has, more will be given, but as for the one who has nothing, even what he has will be taken away'" (v. 26).

Sporting *News* in 2015 chose what it considered to be the ten greatest players in Alabama football history.

Among the ten (named in no particular order) is guard John Hannah. He was a first-team All-American in 1971 and '72.

Linebacker Derrick Thomas made the *News'* list. As a senior in 1988, he lodged an "other-worldly" 27 sacks. He was a unanimous All-America and won the Dick Butkus Award.

The magazine liked Lee Roy Jordan, a linebacker and center for Bear Bryant from 1960-62. In 1962, he was All-America and won the national Lineman of the Year Award. Also among the *News'* top ten is end Ozzie Newsome. In 1977, he was the SEC Lineman of the Year. He was Alabama's Player of the Decade for the 1970s.

On the list is linebacker Cornelius Bennett. In 1986, he was the SEC Player of the Year and won the Lombardi Award. He was a three-time All-American. All-American center Dwight Stephenson (1977-79) is among the ten. Bryant once called him the greatest player he ever coached, regardless of position.

Linebacker Woodrow Lowe made the list. He was a three-time All-American (1973, '74, '75). He still holds the school record for tackles in a season with 134. Wide receivers Julio Jones and Amari Cooper also made the top ten list. Jones set school records that Cooper subsequently broke.

Rounding out the list is running back Mark Ingram, who in 2009 as a unanimous All-American won Alabama's first Heisman Trophy. (Derrick Henry won the award in 2015.)

The ten Alabama football players on this list (and that eleventh player who won the big award) were successful because they made the most of what God gave them. The Bible calls it stewardship.

Jesus preached the same approach through the rather startling parable of the ten minas (think "dollars"). Through that story, our Lord admonishes us that in the time before he returns, we are to use wisely and well the talents, gifts, and resources God has given us.

The pivotal question, of course, is what constitutes "wisely and well." Well, Jesus tells us that, too, in this parable. Our Lord and Savior was so hard on the hapless servant because he was concerned only for himself and his own welfare and thus did nothing to increase his master's wealth.

The analogy is obvious for the believer. We are to use what we have for the benefit of God's Kingdom, to build and to expand it. We are not to sit around on our hands and wait for Christ's glorious return; we are to work for Jesus, the Lord of our life.

What makes guys [like Ozzie Newsome] special? They had talent [and] worked hard. I said, God blessed me and I'm willing to do those things.
— Dwight Stephenson on being a good steward

As good stewards, we are to get up, get out, and get to work for God, using what he has given us.

DAZED & CONFUSED

Read Genesis 11:1-9.

"There the Lord confused the language of the whole world" (v. 9a).

Redshirt freshman Michael Williams was quite confused. He had good reason to be.

As a senior tight end in 2012, Williams caught 24 passes for 183 yards and four touchdowns. "My role wasn't to run down the field and catch 20- or 30-yard passes," he once said. "I got first downs, I got touchdowns, whatever Coach [Nick] Saban asked me to do, that's what I did." Williams did come up with a key touchdown catch in his final game. In the BCS National Championship Game against Notre Dame on Jan. 7, 2013, he caught a 3-yard touchdown pass from A.J. McCarron. That hiked the Alabama lead to 14-0, and the 42-14 rout was on.

Though it ended in glory, Williams' career in Tuscaloosa didn't exactly begin that way. Coming out of a smaller high school, he wasn't ready for the level of conditioning he faced at Alabama. During his first-ever conditioning drill — he passed out. Strength coach Scott Cochran picked him up and told him, "Repeat after me. I'm gonna be great." As the Notre Dame game ended, Cochran looked at Williams and said, "What did I tell you?"

Williams was recruited as a defensive end, which accounts for his confusion at practice one day during his 2008 redshirt season. He trotted out to begin his scout team duties when tight ends coach Bobby Williams came up to him and suddenly barked, "Mike, catch this ball." He caught it. Then the coach said, "Run this way and catch the ball." Williams ran the way he was told to, and again he caught the ball.

The coach didn't say another word, leaving the confused freshman wondering just what in the world all that was about. He found out after practice when he discovered a white jersey in his locker. "From then on," he said, "I was playing tight end."

Though it sometimes doesn't seem that way, confusion is not the natural order of things. God's universe — from the brilliant arrangement of DNA to the complex harmony of a millipede's legs to the dazzling array of the stars — is ordered. God's act of creation was at its most basic the bringing of order out of chaos.

So why then is confusion so pervasive in our society today? Why do so many of us struggle to make sense of our lives, foundering in our confusion over everything from our morals and values to our sexual orientation and our sense of what is right and what is wrong? The lesson of the Tower of Babel is instructive. That which God does not ordain he does not sustain. Thus, confusion is not the problem itself but is rather a symptom of the absence of God's will and God's power in our lives.

Confusion for the children of God is basically a sense of purposelessness. It fills the void in our lives that is created by a lack of intimacy with God.

What's the point of that?
— *Michael Williams after catching passes for the first time at practice*

**In our lives, keeping confusion away
requires keeping God near.**

DAY 47

PROBLEM CHILD

Read James 1:2-12.

"Blessed is the man who perseveres under trial, because when he has stood the test, he will receive the crown of life that God has promised to those who love him" (v. 12).

For the Tide, getting to the 1946 Rose Bowl was a bigger problem that winning the game.

The undefeated national champions of 1945 were led by sophomore quarterback-halfback-defensive back Harry Gilmer. He was an All-American and the SEC Player of the Year.

The 10-0 season earned the team a berth in the school's sixth Rose Bowl, against Southern Cal. Transportation — particularly cross-country — was a problem. The trains were overloaded picking up servicemen on the West Coast and taking them back home on the East Coast. This meant the team had no problem finding seats on a West-bound train. According to Gilmer, they wound up on a 100-car train with 97 vacant cars. All those empty seats would be filled with servicemen on the return trip.

The problem, though, was getting to California speedily. The West-bound train had to pull over and wait for any train heading East with servicemen. Those trains had priorities. Thus, it took the squad four days and three nights to get to Pasadena.

The team had a further problem getting onto the field. In the locker room, head coach Frank Thomas, who, Gilmer said, "made speeches like [Knute] Rockne," launched into one of his famous pep talks. He got louder and louder until he was screaming and topped it off with, "Let's go!"

The fired-up players took off down the narrow tunnel that led to the field and wound up jammed at the closed tunnel door. No one could get the door open! When they finally did, several of the players up front got trampled in the rush.

The game itself was no problem. Alabama won 34-14.

Problems are such a ubiquitous feature of our lives that a whole day — twenty-four hours — without a single problem ranks right up there with a government without taxes, an Alabama team that never, ever loses a game, and entertaining, wholesome television programs. We just can't even imagine it.

But that's life. Even Jesus had his share of problems, especially with his twelve-man staff. Jesus could have easily removed all problems from his daily walk, but what good would that have done us? Our goal is to become like Jesus, and we could never fashion ourselves after a man who didn't encounter job stress, criticism, loneliness, temptation, frustration, and discouragement.

Instead, Jesus showed us that when — not if — problems come, a person of faith uses them to get better rather than letting the problems use him to get bitter. We learn God-filled perseverance and patience as we develop and deepen our faith and our trust in God. Problems will pass; eternity will not.

It didn't matter. We never dreamed of [playing] in the Rose Bowl.
— Harry Gilmer on the problems the team had getting to California

**The problem with problems is that
we often let them use us and become bitter
rather than using them to become better.**

DAY 48

PRAYER WARRIORS

Read Luke 18:1-8.

"Then Jesus told his disciples a parable to show them that they should always pray and not give up" (v. 1).

Trevor Releford threw up a prayer and it was answered. Alabama win.

The 19-11 Tide hosted Georgia on March 9, 2013. Everything went right well early on. Alabama held the Bulldogs scoreless for more than 8 minutes in the first half and scored thirteen straight points during that stretch. That let the home team take a 32-18 lead into the locker room at the break.

But the Bulldogs rallied to set up a frenzied finish. They hit a free throw and a trey to tie the game at 58 with 48 seconds left. Then to the horror of the home fans, Georgia forced a turnover that had a Bulldog driving for the basket as the clock ticked down.

There was contact that left the Georgia player and sophomore forward Nick Jacobs sprawled on the floor, but no foul was called. When the ball bounced free, sophomore forward Rodney Cooper scooped it up.

He spotted Releford, a junior guard, sprinting downcourt and wide open. Releford would finish in 2013-14 as Alabama's all-time leader in steals and fourth all-time in scoring. He would earn All-SEC first-team honors twice.

With two seconds on the clock, Cooper whipped the ball to Releford. He caught it, dribbled a couple of times, and let fly with his prayer a few feet short of midcourt. His 50-footer was "straight, true and just long enough."

Alabama had a 61-58 win. After Releford was swamped by his teammates in a wild celebration, he admitted that he never even practiced half-court shots. He evidently didn't have to.

To speak of Trevor Releford's buzzer-beater as a "prayer" is to say it had only a slight chance of going in. That's an interesting definition for Christians. As people of faith, we know there is every chance our prayers will be heard and answered.

Any problems we may have with prayer and its results derive from our side, not God's. We pray for a while about something – perhaps fervently at first – but our enthusiasm wanes if we don't receive the answer we want exactly when we want it. Why waste our time by asking for the same thing over and over again?

But God isn't deaf; God does hear our prayers, and God does respond to them. As Jesus clearly taught, our prayers have an impact because they turn the power of Almighty God loose in this world. Thus, falling to our knees and praying to God is not a sign of weakness and helplessness. Rather, praying for someone or something is an aggressive act, an intentional ministry, a conscious and fervent attempt on our part to change someone's life or the world for the better.

God responds to our prayers; we often just can't perceive or don't understand how he is working to make those prayers come about.

I knew it was on target, but I thought it was going to be a little bit short.
— Trevor Releford on his game-winning prayer vs. Georgia

Jesus taught us to always pray and never give up.

GIFT-WRAPPED

Read James 1:13-18.

"Every good and perfect gift is from above, coming down from the Father of the heavenly lights" (v. 17).

Joe Namath turned down a gift; Bear Bryant received one.

The Orange Bowl of Jan. 1, 1965, remains among the most controversial losses in Alabama history. Texas wound up with a 21-17 upset over the top-ranked Tide. In the game's closing seconds, senior quarterback Joe Namath apparently scored. One official even signaled "touchdown." Another official, however, said, "No score." The refs got together, talked it over, and ruled Texas had stopped Alabama short of the goal line.

On the sideline, a disappointed Namath, who was the game's MVP, took a drink of water, threw the cup on the ground, and bellowed, "I know I scored!" Bryant ordered him into the dressing room. "If you can't jam it in from there without leaving any doubt, you don't deserve to win," he said.

Prior to the game, Bryant and Namath had met with Sonny Werblin, the owner of the New York Jets. Namath agreed to sign a contract that would make him the highest paid player in pro football history. All the contact with the Jets was in strict accordance with the rules of the day.

Everything was in such "strict accordance" with the rules that Namath refused Werblin's offer of a gift. He said Bryant had told him not to accept anything until after the game had been played.

Just what was that big gift? A Coca-Cola.

A few weeks after the Orange Bowl, Bryant himself received a gift from the Jets owner, who was appreciative of the coach's help with Namath. Assistant coach Clem Gryska recalled that Werblin sent the Bear some hats. He had noticed Bryant wearing Fedoras, "the elegant ones with the rim and the feather on them."

The Bear took an immediate liking to those hats. They were houndstooth.

Receiving a gift is nice, but giving has its pleasures too, doesn't it? The children's excitement on Christmas morning. That smile of pure delight on your spouse's face when you came up with a really cool anniversary present. Your dad's surprise that time you didn't give him a tie or socks. There really does seem to be something to this being more blessed to give than to receive.

No matter how generous we may be, though, we are grumbling misers compared to God, who is the greatest gift-giver of all. That's because all the good things in our lives — every one of them — come from God. Friends, love, health, family, the air we breathe, the sun that warms us, even our very lives are all gifts from a profligate God. And here's the kicker: He even gives us eternal life with him through the gift of his son.

What in the world can we possibly give God in return? Our love and our life.

I offered him a Coca-Cola and he refused.
— A flabbergasted Sonny Werblin to a reporter about Joe Namath

Nobody can match God when it comes to giving,
but you can give him the gift of your love
in appreciation.

DAY 50

GIVE IT UP

Read Luke 9:57-62.

"'No one who puts his hand to the plow and looks back is fit for service in the kingdom of God" (v.62).

The Crimson Tide beat Notre Dame in the 2012 BCS title game in large part because of the most basic of football reasons: Alabama's offensive line bludgeoned the Irish into submission.

Fighting Irish head coach Brian Kelly had it right the day before the game of Jan. 7, 2013, in Miami. He declared, "I still think this game is going to be decided by what happens up front." What happened up front was that in the face of Alabama's relentless and remorseless offensive line, "the Notre Dame defense did its best imitation of butter."

Alabama's dominance up front was revealed on the Tide's first possession. Tailback Eddie Lacy ran 20 yards for the game's initial touchdown, ripping through "a Hummer-sized hole created by All-American left guard Chance Warmack."

On its first possession of the second half, Alabama drove 97 yards for a touchdown and a 35-0 lead. On the scoring play, quarterback A.J. McCarron took the snap and set up on the left side behind Warmack, tackle Cyrus Kouandjio, and tight end Michael Williams. He "stood there like a man waiting for a bus" while wide receiver Amari Cooper ran a deep crossing pattern. Finally, still untouched, McCarron delivered a strike to Cooper.

The line's total dominance was especially remarkable since

All-American center Barrett Jones played with a torn ligament in his left foot.

After the game, head coach Nick Saban said that the O-line, which also included guard Anthony Steen, tackle D.J. Fluker, and tight end Kelly Johnson, "may be the best [bunch] . . . that we've ever had or been associated with." They sure looked it while they pummelled the Irish into submission.

Why in the world would anyone reject Jesus Christ after hearing his message of hope and resurrection? Folks do, but we really shouldn't be too hard on our contemporaries. After all, Luke tells us that at least a couple of men were willing to follow Jesus, but only with conditions. And they saw, heard, and looked into the eyes of the walking, talking, living Christ!

Christianity is difficult for so many because Jesus demands submission. That means we have to give up control of our lives; we have to turn them over to God. For too many people, that is too scary to seriously consider. After all, we know better than God does. That explains why so many people become Christians only after their lives have become shipwrecks. They are out of options; God is a last resort, so why not give him a try?

Yes, following Jesus involves cost. The cross comes with the crown; the flip side of mercy is judgment. But it is also true that only with Jesus can we live in the joy that God intends for us.

He called it. He just couldn't do anything about it.
— ESPN's Ivan Maisel on Brian Kelly's saying the title game would be
won up front

Submission to God only appears to be losing;
it is winning in the greatest, most complete way.

DAY 51

SHOW ME

Read 1 Corinthians 2:6-16.

*"[W]e speak of God's secret wisdom . . . that has been
hidden. . . . [B]ut God has revealed it to us by his Spirit"
(vv. 7, 10a).*

Jay Barker had a revelation, and Alabama fans will forever be
grateful for it.

In 1992, Barker quarterbacked the Tide to the national championship as a sophomore. The season concluded with the legendary
34-13 waxing of Miami in the Sugar Bowl.

That '92 season was built on the backs of an overpowering defense that ranked first in the nation. The 1993 season, however,
was different. All-American cornerback Antonio Langham understood it when he observed, "We aren't going to go out now and
dominate [on defense] from start to finish."

That meant additional pressure on the offense, especially for
Barker. As head coach Gene Stallings noted, "How many times
can you beat Miami . . . when you throw for only 18 yards?" His
point was clear; in '93, Alabama would take the field with a new
quarterback or an improved Barker, who admitted that sometimes
during the '92 season "I didn't know what I was doing."

The choice became moot during the off-season when Barker,
a devout Christian and a tireless worker, had what he called his
"revelation." It came to him during the summer after hours of film
study. Suddenly, he could see the whole field, and, thus, he said,

"I'm more able to understand what this position is all about."

During the '93 season, Stallings said he had never seen a player improve as fast as Barker did. He led the Tide to a 35-2-1 record over his three seasons as a starter. In 1994, he won the Johnny Unitas Golden Arm Award (which honors production on the field and character off it) and finished fifth in the Heisman vote.

Christianity is a revealed religion. We know what we know because God has chosen to reveal it to us. Daniel 2:47 characterizes God as the "revealer of mysteries."

In some cases God reveals specific information to individuals, but generally his revelations are about himself. The supreme revelation, of course, is Jesus Christ, as disclosed in the Gospels.

The New Testament is replete with audacious claims, but perhaps none is more astounding than Paul's declaration in v. 16 that "we have the mind of Christ." Ponder that a moment. When you live in a personal relationship with Jesus, you know all about him, even his mind. Christ thus reveals to you personally what he revealed to those he associated with when he walked this Earth: the very mind of God.

Revelation isn't prophecy for most of us, and it isn't limited to the chosen few. Instead, revelation through the Holy Spirit achieved by our faith in Christ is the means God provides for us to learn his will for our lives. Our task is to put that revealed knowledge to use for the betterment of God's kingdom.

It was like going from tunnel vision to seeing everything.
— Jay Barker on his revelation in the summer of '93

**As startling as it sounds, faith in Jesus grants
you the privilege of access to the mind of God.**

DAY 52

STRANGE BUT TRUE

Read Philippians 2:1-11.

"And being found in appearance as a man, he humbled himself and became obedient to death – even death on a cross!" (v. 7)

Landon Collins announced his decision as to where he would play college football and touched off one of the strangest such sessions ever.

On Jan. 5, 2012, Collins, a five-star safety from Louisiana, told the country of his decision in a live TV broadcast. Having previously narrowed his choices to Alabama and LSU, he quickly put an Alabama cap on and declared, "Roll, Tide!"

Then the show turned strange. Fifteen family members and friends on stage with Collins did just as folks usually do on such occasions: They applauded. From his mother, though, Collins received only a scowl of displeasure. She didn't clap, she didn't smile, and she proceeded to openly voice her disapproval of her son's decision, going so far as to shout, "Go, Tigers."

On National Signing Day, she threatened not to sign Collins' letter of intent for Alabama. "I was 2 minutes from ripping them up," she said. "I really wasn't going to sign them."

But Landon and his brother, Gerald, ganged up on her and persuaded her to go along with them — with a pinkie swear. Her son promised and then gave the pinkie swear that he would "do well in class and play hard." She knew Landon kept his promises and told him, "Play hard or don't come home." Then "I took a deep breath and walked down the stairs and signed his life away to Alabama, even though I hated it," she said.

Collins did indeed keep his promise. He became a starter as a sophomore in 2013. Then in 2014, he led the team with 98 tackles and was an All-American. He entered the NFL draft in 2015.

Some things in life are so strange their existence can't really be explained. How else can we account for the sport of curling, tofu, that people go to bars hoping to meet the "right" person, the proliferation of tattoos, and the behavior of teenagers? Isn't it strange that someone would hear the life-changing message of salvation in Jesus Christ and then walk away from it?

And how strange is that plan of salvation that God has for us? Just consider what God did. He could have come roaring down, annihilating everyone whose sinfulness offended him, which, of course, is pretty much all of us. Then he could have brushed off his hands, nodded the divine head, and left a scorched planet in his wake. All in a day's work.

Instead, God came up with a totally novel plan: He would save the world by becoming a human being, letting himself be humiliated, tortured, and killed, thus establishing a kingdom of justice and righteousness that will last forever.

It's a strange way to save the world — but it's true.

Landon Collins committed to Alabama in one of the strangest announcements ever recorded on national television.
— ESPN SEC reporter Alex Scarborough

It's strange but true: God allowed himself to be killed on a cross to save the world.

STORY TIME

Read Luke 8:26-39.

*"'Return home and tell how much God has done for you.'
So the man went away and told all over town how much
Jesus had done for him" (v. 39).*

Years later, Jenny Mainz still tells her teams the story of a pair
of running shoes.

In June 1997, Mainz left a coaching position at Iowa to take
charge of the women's tennis program at Bama. She met her prospective team during her interview and liked what she saw. The
team she saw at her interview, however, wasn't the one that she
wound up coaching. Several players either left or were sidelined
with injuries. "Everything sort of unraveled," Mainz said.

It unraveled in a big way. To get enough bodies to field a team,
the new coach had to scour sororities and physical education
classes. She eventually assembled a squad with four scholarship
players and four walk-ons. They went 0-21.

It got a little better in 1999 with a 3-18 record and in 2000 with
a 7-15 slate. But the most glaring statistic of all was an 0-36 record
against SEC competition. Athletic director Mal Moore noticed.
He called Mainz into his office and told her, "You know, I like you,
but you gotta win, and you gotta win in the conference."

As Mainz put it, "By the grace of God, it happened." That and
a little help from a pair of running shoes. Prior to the first SEC
match of the 2001 season, a Mainz nervous about her future went

to lunch with assistant coach Dave Anderson. He said, "Boss, when we win tomorrow, I'm going to have my running shoes by the door. As soon as we win, I'm getting those running shoes and I'm going on a run."

Alabama won 6-1, Anderson went for his run, and Mainz has been solid as the Alabama coach ever since. Each season she shares the story of the running shoes and her coach's assurance to emphasize the supportive atmosphere the team must have.

So you've never successfully coached an SEC team as Jenny Mainz has. You nevertheless have a story to tell; it's the story of your life and it's unique. No one else among the billions of people on this planet can tell the same story.

Part of that story is your encounter with Jesus. It's the most important chapter of anyone's life, but all too often believers in Jesus Christ don't tell it. Otherwise brave and daring Christian men and women who wouldn't think twice about skydiving or whitewater rafting often quail when faced with the prospect of speaking about Jesus to someone else. It's the dreaded "W" word: witness. "I just don't know what to say," we sputter.

But witnessing is nothing but telling your story. No one can refute it; no one can claim it isn't true. You don't get into some great theological debate for which you're ill prepared. You just tell the beautiful, awesome story of Jesus and you.

The story behind the running shoes is synonymous with the team culture [Jenny Mainz] tries to create in her locker room.
— The Crimson White's *Kayla Montgomery*

We all have a story to tell, but the most important part of all is the chapter where we meet Jesus.

DAY 54

ONE-MAN ARMY

Read Revelation 19:11-21.

"The rest of them were killed by the sword that came out of the mouth of the rider on the horse" (v. 21).

A battle of unbeatens on national television was to be a chance for LSU's quarterback to shine. Instead, an unheralded Alabama field general was practically a one-man army.

Alabama-LSU showdowns are not a new phenomenon. On Nov. 11, 1972, in Birmingham, an 8-0 Tide team took on a 7-0 LSU team. The game was considered an "ideal showcase" for LSU's senior signal-caller, Bert Jones.

On the other side of the ball was Alabama senior Terry Davis, "too small for the pros" and with "arm and statistics [that] are ungodlike." What he could do was run the wishbone offense.

Though Alabama had thrown only three times — with no completions — in a 14-7 defeat of LSU in 1971, Bear Bryant insisted that Davis could pass well enough. In the '72 clash of the Titans, he did just that. And practically everything else.

Davis "passed and ran and pitched and faked and handed off, and just generally executed" so well that LSU didn't know what to expect. The Tigers took the early lead with a Jones touchdown toss, but then Davis threw a 25-yard scoring pass to wide receiver Wayne Wheeler. 7-7. Early in the second half, he hit Wheeler again, this time for a 29-yard catch-and-run TD. 14-7. Minutes later, he swept around his end for a 25-yard touchdown run. 21-7.

LSU cut the lead the 21-14, but Davis led the Tide on a 78-yard drive, all on the ground. He had 42 of the yards himself. 28-14. Game over. Alabama went on to win 35-21.

Davis did indeed "pass well enough." He passed so well that LSU had to adjust its defense. Then Davis simply took charge of the wishbone's running game, and LSU was done.

A lot of folks eventually found out about Bama's unheralded quarterback. Davis finished fifth in the Heisman voting.

A situation similar to a one-man army will occur when Christ returns. He will not come back to us as the meek lamb led unprotestingly to slaughter on the cross. Instead, he will be a conquering one-man army on a white horse who will destroy the forces responsible for disorder and chaos in God's world.

This image of our Jesus as a warrior may well shock and discomfort us; it should also excite and thrill us. It reminds us vividly that God will unleash his awesome power to effect justice and righteousness in a world that persecutes his people and slanders his name. It should also lend us a sense of urgency because the time will pass when decisions for Christ can still be made.

For now, Jesus has an army at his disposal in the billions of Christians around the world. We are Christian soldiers; we have a world to conquer for our Lord — before he returns as a one-man army to finish the job.

I don't know how you get consideration for that Heisman, but Terry Davis hasn't lost a regular season game.
    — Bear Bryant on his one-man army after the LSU game

Jesus will return as a one-man army to conquer the forces of evil; for now, we are his army.

DAY 55

ON TOP OF THE WORLD

Read Matthew 16:24-27.

"What good will it be for a man if he gains the whole world, yet forfeits his soul?" (v. 16a)

In 1961, Bear Bryant was on top of the world.

He was successful. When the Bear arrived in Tuscaloosa, Alabama had won two games in the last two seasons. In his third season, 1960, he had the Tide ranked in the top ten. In 1961, Alabama went undefeated and won the national championship. The team built its success on its defense, surrendering a grand total of 25 points the whole season.

The Bear was already famous in 1961. *Sports Illustrated* declared him to be the best football coach in the country "because of his fierce energy and intelligence and dedication." He had his own television show on Sundays during football season. His face was on outdoor advertising signs around Birmingham, and no one could "drink a Coke in Alabama without looking at Bear Bryant."

Though coy about his finances, Bryant was at least borderline rich in 1961. The powers that be were thinking about paying their new coach $30,000 to $40,000 when they hired him away from Texas A&M. Instead, Bryant asked how much money the school president made. He was told $17,500. "Then I'll take that," he said. "I'll have enough trouble with the faculty as it is."

Nevertheless, he lived in a sprawling home and rode in an air-conditioned Cadillac complete with a chauffeur. He was on the board of two companies and had an interest in several building projects. He was widely known to have made a bunch of money on the stock market thanks to tips from some wealthy boosters. Bear Bryant had it all: success, fame, and wealth. But the Alabama legend was successful at another level, too. He knew that all the world's baubles and everything he had then and would accumulate in the future would not buy him a home in Heaven. That came only through his faith in Jesus Christ.

Prosperity and fame in a lifetime are no indication of God's favor, though some preachers warp the gospel to assert they are. If you really want to know what God thinks of money, look at many of the people he gives it to. Neither are poverty and anonymity indications of God's displeasure. Jesus hung out with the poor and the dispossessed, not the rich and the powerful.

The riches, the accolades, and the esteem of this world have no value in God's eyes. That does not in turn apply to those who have them. Christians need money to support missionaries, charities, and their local churches. Spreading the gospel takes money and influence. Fame doesn't hurt either.

The problem comes when we seek success, fame, and wealth instead of searching out God's favor. Then we truly have gained the world and lost our soul.

For a man supposed to have as much money as I do, I owe more people than anyone I know.
— *Bear Bryant, denying in 1961 that he was a millionaire*

**Our wealth, fame, and success are worthwhile
in God's sight only when they are used
to advance his kingdom.**

DAY 56

SOMETHING NEW

Read Ephesians 4:17-24.

"You were taught . . . to put off your old self . . . and to put on the new self, created to be like God in true righteousness and holiness" (vv. 22, 24).

Alabama sprang something brand new on West Virginia, and the Mountaineers weren't ready for it.

Over the years, Bama's Nick Saban has not exactly been a big fan of hurry-up offenses. He has quite gladly described Alabama's offense and play-calling as being "like the dinosaur age."

Writer Michael Casagrande of *AL.com* said that the no-huddle-hurry-up offenses frustrate Alabama's head coach because "they eliminate real-time coaching and the ability to substitute." Saban has expressed his displeasure with the no-huddles by calling for study into the medical effect of the extra exposure to injury the players receive with them.

So with that background and Alabama's legacy of a "dinosaur-age" offense, West Virginia was caught flat-footed in 2014's season opener. Late in the first half, the Tide suddenly switched to a no-huddle, hurry-up offense.

With new offensive coordinator Lane Kiffin on board, the team had been quietly working on the offense through the summer. With the score tied at 10, Saban noticed that quarterback Blake Sims, making his first start, was "a little bit rattled." So after a short run, the Tide didn't huddle up. Sims used only 18 seconds before getting the ball and hitting Amari Cooper for a first down.

"They looked kind of surprised," Sims said about the reaction from the Mountaineers. Seeing as how they had no film on the new look and Alabama had said nothing about it, WVU's befuddlement was understandable.

Saban used the hurry-up offense effectively on into the third quarter. Bama ran 82 plays — after averaging 63.5 snaps in 2013 — and whipped West Virginia 33-23. Saban called West Virginia's offense "fast ball," but on this night of a new wrinkle to the Tide's offense, it wasn't fast enough.

New things in our lives often have a life-changing effect. A new spouse. A new baby. A new job. Even something as mundane as a new television set or lawn mower jolts us with change.

While new experiences, new people, and new toys may make our lives new, they can't make new lives for us. Inside, where it counts – down in the deepest recesses of our soul – we're still the same, no matter how desperately we may wish to change.

An inner restlessness drives us to seek escape from a life that is a monotonous routine. Such a mundane existence just isn't good enough for someone who is a child of God; it can't even be called living. We want more out of life; something's got to change.

The only hope for a new life lies in becoming a brand new man or woman. And that is possible only through Jesus Christ, he who can make all things new again.

It was something we hadn't ever done before, so it helped us out a lot.
— Blake Sims on Alabama's hurry-up offense vs. West Virginia

**A brand new you with the promise
of a life worth living is waiting in Jesus Christ.**

DAY 57

HOPE CHEST

Read Psalm 42.

"Put your hope in God, for I will yet praise him, my Savior and my God" (v. 5b).

The Florida Gators still had a wee bit of hope. But then the Alabama defense got together during a timeout.

On the evening of Oct. 1, 2011, in Gainesville, Fla., the 4-0 Tide did battle with the 4-0 and 12th-ranked Gators. The game got off to a rollicking start for the home team. Less than ten minutes into the first quarter, Florida had ridden the SEC's best offense to a 10-3 lead.

Evidently, the Gators had some realistic hopes of pulling off the upset against a defense described as "the most fearsome unit in college football." Nah. The home team didn't know it, but its side of the scoreboard wouldn't change again.

Florida's hopes headed south with a 5-yard touchdown run from Trent Richardson and a 45-yard TD interception return by All-American linebacker Courtney Upshaw. It was 17-10.

The Gators were still hanging on with 8:44 to go in the second quarter. They were at their own 14, still hoping as they waited out a timeout. Unfortunately for them, Alabama defensive coordinator Kirby Smart had his charges circled about him, giving them some last-gasp instructions. When they trotted back onto the field, all hope was gone.

The series went like this: 1) feeble pass because of rush from nosetackle Josh Chapman; 2) 1-yard loss on run, tackle by Damion Square; 3) incomplete pass, hit by safety Will Lowery. Punt.

Ten plays later, A.J. McCarron dived into the end zone. All hope was gone, because "there doesn't appear to be an offense in the land that can rally from a two-touchdown deficit" against Bama's defense. Florida sure couldn't. Alabama won 38-10.

Only when a life has no hope does it become not worth the living. To hope is not merely to want something; that is desire or wishful thinking. To produce hope, desire must be coupled with some degree of expectation.

Therein lies the great problem. We may wish for a million dollars, relief from our diabetes, world peace, or a way to lose weight while stuffing ourselves with doughnuts, cheeseburgers, and fried chicken. Our hopes, however, must be firmly grounded, or they will inevitably lead us to disappointment, shame, and disaster. In other words, false hopes ruin us.

One of the most basic issues of our lives, therefore, becomes discovering or locating that in which we can place our hope. Where can we find sure promises for a future that we can count on? Where can we place our hope with realistic expectations that we can live securely even though some of the promises we rely on are yet to be delivered?

In God. In God and God alone lies our hope.

At this moment on a cool and breezy evening, there was still a thread of hope for [Florida].
— *SI's Lars Anderson at the 8:44 mark of the second quarter*

God and his sustaining power are the source of the only meaningful hope possible in our lives.

DAY 58

TRUE CHAMPIONS

Read 1 Corinthians 9:24-27.

"Everyone who competes in the games goes into strict training. . . . [W]e do it to get a crown that will last forever" (v. 25).

Senior Brooke Pancake knew it was her time before she hit it. "It" was a four-foot putt that made champions out of the Alabama women's golf team for the first time.

Pancake is one of Alabama's most decorated athletes. From 2008-12, she was All-SEC four times and All-America three times. She won the Honda Award in 2012 as the top collegiate player in the nation. That same year, she was the Capital One Academic All-American of the Year and the SEC's Female Athlete of the Year.

In the spring of 2012, the Alabama team earned its seventh straight bid to the 72-hole NCAA championship tournament. It was one of the tightest competitions in history with only four strokes separating the top four teams the last day.

Two-time NCAA champion Southern Cal was the favorite, but the Tide came out hot. Alabama led the Trojans by 14 strokes after 36 holes. The third day, though, USC closed to within two strokes, setting up a nail-biting final day.

As the last 18 holes played out, Alabama seemed to have fallen out of the competition. Teeing off at No. 16, Alabama sophomore Hannah Collier looked up at the leaderboard and saw that the Tide trailed the Trojans by five strokes. "What's left to lose?" she thought. "Might as well swing freely, which [head coach] Mic [Potter] tells me to do." With that all-or-nothing approach, she birdied 17 and 18 to propel Alabama back into the lead.

Southern Cal pulled to within a stroke on the final hole with Pancake needing a par to pull out the win. Her birdie putt from 60 feet lipped the cup before going four feet past the hole. "This is my moment," she thought as she stood over her par putt.

She confidently knocked it home. They were champions.

Alabama's 2012 golf national championship is an apt metaphor for the life we lead as Christians. When it seemed their hopes had been dashed and their faith in themselves had been misplaced, they stayed on course and kept battling.

Such is the life of a Christian. It is a wonderful life — the only really worthwhile one — but it isn't necessarily an easy life. Paul spoke of beating his body and making it a slave; that's certainly not very appealing. No, the well-lived Christian life today requires a keen sense of purpose, discipline, hard work, and preparation. Which sounds a lot like a championship team in any sport.

Very few of us get the chance to compete for an NCAA national title. All of us, however, who put our faith in Jesus Christ, compete for a championship. Instead of a trophy, we receive a crown. Instead of sycophantic adulation, we earn God's pleasure and a nod of approval from Jesus Christ.

We are true champions — for all of eternity.

I can't think of a better way to finish my senior year.
— Brooke Pancake on winning the national championship

**Those who follow Christ all the way to Heaven
are life's true champions.**

DAY 59

CHILD'S PLAY

Read Romans 8:9-17.

"[T]hose who are led by the Spirit of God are sons of God"
(v. 14).

Paul Bryant had such a stark childhood that little was expected of him.

The child who would become a legend was born in 1913 and grew up in rural Arkansas in a place called Moro Bottom. He once said it was just "a little piece of bottom land on the Moro Creek about seven miles south of Fordyce." "Life was day to day and hand to mouth" for young Bryant. "It was a burden on everybody back in that time to make a living," said Ray Bryant, a grand-nephew of the Bear.

Paul was the eleventh of twelve children. He often accompanied his mother into town on a wagon pulled by a mule. They rode into Fordyce to sell what they produced, everything "from milk and eggs to turnips and watermelon." Ray Bryant recalled that during winter's coldest weather, Paul would heat some bricks in the fireplace and put them in the bed of the wagon to keep their feet warm.

The reception in town was rough on young Paul. They had to ride by the high school on their trips to market, and a lot of the kids made fun of them, their wagon, their produce, and their poverty. Ray Bryant said that what bothered Paul most of all was that they also made fun of his mama.

When Bryant left to play football for Alabama, practically nobody in Fordyce thought he'd stick with it. He almost quit more then once, especially when his father died and his mother was having a hard time. He wrote a cousin he was coming home. The cousin wired back, "Go ahead and quit, just like everybody predicted you would." It was the right thing to say. "I wasn't about to quit after that," Bryant said.

As was the case with Bear Bryant, childhood is often not the idyllic time we imagine it to be for the world's youngsters. The circumstances can be less than desirable even when the parent or parents honestly do the best they can for their children.

In his role as the creator of all life, God is in a sense the father of us all. Jesus, however, added a new layer of meaning to the traditional understanding of our relationship with God that truly renders us his children. Since only Christ is God's true son, only through Christ's mediation for us with God can the parent-child relationship be our own.

Our vision of a perfect childhood includes growth in a warm, safe, loving environment wherein the parent cherishes, protects, nurtures, and teaches the child. Love both restrains and guides the parent's power, which otherwise may lead to abuse.

In other words, our conception of a perfect childhood matches God's vision for our relationship with him through Jesus.

His father was a sickly man [and] the family was poor.
— Writer Don Wade on Bear Bryant's childhood

The physical act of birth renders us a child
of our parents; the spiritual act of receiving Jesus
Christ as our Lord renders us a child of God.

DAY 60

FANCY FOOTWORK

Read Isaiah 52:7-12.

"How beautiful on the mountains are the feet of those who bring good news" (v. 7).

Here's the rule: Football requires two feet. Here's the exception: Barrett Jones.

Jones is "perhaps the most decorated player in Alabama football history." In addition to a number of other awards, he was a two-time All-America, at tackle in 2011 and at center in 2012. All the accolades, though, were secondary to him. "I want to be known as a Christian who happens to play football, not a football player who happens to be a Christian," he has said. "My faith is just not another thing that I do. It's who I am. It is my identity."

About those feet. Late in the first quarter of the 32-28 win over Georgia in the 2012 SEC Championship Game, Jones was making a block and "everything in the middle of my foot just popped and tore." He kept on playing, telling the doctors at halftime that he had sprained his foot "a little bit." It wasn't the truth and he knew it. "It was probably the most pain I've ever had in a game," he said.

Despite the pain caused by what was obviously an injury far more serious than a sprain, Jones didn't miss a play at center. He helped open holes for backs Eddie Lacy and T.J. Yeldon and a rushing attack that rolled up 350 yards.

Jones' injury was diagnosed as a ligament tear. In other words, he had played against Georgia on one foot. He rehabbed as much as he could during the long layoff before the national championship game against Notre Dame, but only surgery would heal the damage and stop the pain.

Still, Jones insisted on playing. Since he had only one good foot, he had to change his blocking techniques. "I didn't play great but I played all right," he said. Yes, he did. The Tide rolled up 265 yards rushing in destroying the Irish for the national title.

Day to day, we rarely pay much attention to our feet. Throw athlete's foot, corns, calluses, bunions, or ingrown toenails into the mix, however, and those aching digits make us a whole lot more aware of them and how important they are.

Even if we are flattered when someone tells us how lovely certain of our body parts are, we probably would regard as slightly strange someone's commenting on how pretty and delectable our feet are. Especially if we're men and don't have the advantage of painted toenails.

But even Jehovah himself waxes poetic about our pretty feet under one circumstance: when we are hotfooting about delivering the good news of salvation through Jesus Christ. We are commissioned by our Lord to put those feet — flat or otherwise — onto the ground and share with others God's life-changing message of redemption through Christ.

The feet of the gospel's messenger are beautiful because they bear the bearer of the most beautiful message of all: Jesus saves.

I just didn't have much power in that foot.
— Barrett Jones on playing on one foot vs. Notre Dame

Our feet are beautiful when they take us to people who need the message of salvation in Jesus.

DAY 61

THE SCARS

Read John 20:19-31.

*"'Put your finger here; see my hands. Reach out your
hand and put it into my side. Stop doubting and believe'"
(v. 27).*

Nico Johnson bears the scars of an act of selfless love. He also
bears the burdens of a pair of life-altering losses.

Johnson stood at the summit of his college career. In his final
game, he was about to play Notre Dame for the third national title
in his four seasons in Tuscaloosa. He should have been exuberant
and overjoyed. Instead, "I'm just devastated," he said.

That was because he hadn't "even really had time to grieve."
Hundreds of miles away in Andalusia, Ala., they were burying
Duke, the man without whom Johnson would never have been
where he was. Durrell "Duke" Smith was Johnson's uncle, a
"larger than life man with full, open arms." He had "the biggest
heart in Andalusia," and it gave way on him. He was 53.

Duke ran the Andalusia Sports Complex. Nico ran there after
school each day to escape the fate of so many young people in
his town. Youth like his older brother who was arrested before
he was 14. At the complex, Nico "found hope and guidance" with
Duke. He lifted weights and listened to Duke and pushed himself
to become one of the best linebackers in the country.

Along with Duke, young Nico had his mother, Mamie. As he
grew up, so did his love and respect for her grow. He was 15 when

he walked into the house one day and found her on the floor with complications from her diabetes. One of the reasons he chose Alabama was so he could be close to her.

Then in the spring of 2010, the diabetes finally got the best of Johnson's mother. "I was lost," he said. Only weeks of counsel from Alabama conditioning director Scott Cochran kept Johnson from walking away from everything, including football.

Ultimately Johnson went on, carrying his pain and his scars right on into the NFL. About those scars. They were on his chest because his mother had had a dangerous in-vitro procedure while she was carrying him. She risked her life to keep her son safe.

You have scars too. That car wreck left a good one. So did that bicycle crash. Maybe we better not talk about that time you said, "Hey, watch this!" Your scars are part of your life story, the residue of the pain you've encountered. People's scars are so unique and ubiquitous they're used to identify bodies.

Even Jesus proved who he was by the scars in his hands and in his side. How interesting it is that even after his resurrection, Jesus bore the scars of the pain he endured. Apparently, he bears them still even as he sits upon his throne in Heaven. Why would he even have them in the first place? Why would he, who had all the power in the universe, submit meekly to being tortured and slaughtered?

He did it for you. Jesus' scars tell the story of his love for you.

Mamie raised him well. He has an inner strength he never knew he had.
— Strength coach Scott Cochran on Nico Johnson

In your scars lie stories; the same is true for Jesus,
whose scars tell of his love for you.

DAY 62

FAMILY TRADITION

Read Mark 7:1-13.

"You have let go of the commands of God and are holding on to the traditions of men" (v. 8).

Joe Namath showed up and a tradition crumbled.

Namath, of course, is a Crimson Tide legend. He came to Alabama in 1961 at a time when Bryant was rebuilding the Tide into a national power. From 1962-64, he quarterbacked Alabama to a 29-4 record and the 1964 national championship.

With assistant coach Howard Schnellenberger at his side (See Devotion No. 93.), the recruit arrived splendiferously at the Tide practice field in 1961. Namath showed up wearing a blue straw hat with a feather; there was a pearl somewhere, too.

Bryant was atop his legendary tower. Rumor said that maybe the university president and perhaps one of Bryant's favorite comics had been allowed up there one time each. But nobody else — ever. It was tradition. On this day, though, the Bear leaned over the rail, looked down at his peacocked recruit, and bellowed through his bullhorn, "Send that kid up here."

Namath dutifully climbed up for a brief talk. Encountering Bryant's "authentic Southern gibberish" for the first time, the kid understood little of what he heard. They shook hands, and then Namath "in all his teenage feathered splendor, climbed down and repaired to a waiting Cadillac."

"Who was that?" asked freshman center Gaylon McCollough.

He got his answer from a graduate assistant who had just seen the death of a tradition and had felt the ground shift beneath his feet because Bryant had "invited Yankee Doodle Dandy into his sacred cockpit." That's your new quarterback," he barked.

You encounter traditions practically everywhere in your life. Alabama has them. So does your workplace. Your family may have a particular way of decorating the Christmas tree, or it may gather to celebrate Easter at a certain family member's home.

Your church undoubtedly has traditions also. A particular type of music, for instance. Or how often you celebrate Communion. Or the order of worship.

Jesus knew all about religious tradition; after all, he grew up in the Church. He understood, though, the danger that lay in allowing tradition to become a religion in and of itself, and in his encounter with the Pharisees, Jesus rebuked them for just that.

Jesus changed everything that the world had ever known about faith. This included the traditions that had gradually arisen to define the way the Jews of his day worshipped. Jesus declared that those who truly worship God do not do so by simply observing various traditions, but rather by establishing a meaningful, deep-seated personal relationship with him.

Tradition in our faith life is useful only when it helps to draw us closer to God.

The assistant snorted in disgust, appalled by these changing times [and] by traditions crumbling before [his] eyes.
— *Writer Richard Hoffer on the reaction to Joe Namath's tower climb*

Religious tradition has value only when it serves to strengthen our relationship with God.

DAY 63

BIG DEAL

Read Ephesians 3:1-13.

"His intent was that now, through the church, the manifold wisdom of God should be made known" (v. 10).

What the Alabama pitching staff did in a three-game series against Mississippi Valley State in 2014 was such a really big deal that it made history.

The Tide was expected to whip the Delta Devils of the Southwestern Athletic Conference. Thus, when Alabama won the series opener 8-0 on Friday, March 8, it didn't seem like such a big deal. Junior Spencer Turnbull pitched seven strong innings, giving up only three hits.

On Saturday, though, history was made. For the first time since World War II, the Tide pitchers threw a nine-hitting no-hitter. On April 24, 1942, Eddie Owcar beat Ole Miss 8-0. Against Mississippi Valley State, Justin Kamplain, Jay Shaw, and Geoffrey Bramblett combined to throw the no-hitter in a 7-0 win.

As if that wasn't history enough, in the Sunday finale, the Tide turned the weekend into an even bigger deal. Junior Jon Keller allowed only one hit and had seven strikeouts in six innings of shutout work. Sophomore Ray Castillo pitched a pair of scoreless innings before second baseman Kyle Overstreet made his first pitching appearance of the season. He tossed a scoreless ninth to complete the shutout and earn the save. Alabama won 3-0.

Check those scores: 8-0, 7-0, and 3-0. Mississippi Valley did not score a single run all weekend. That feat -- shutting out an opponent for an entire three-game series -- had not been accomplished by the Tide since way back in 1912. In the first series of the season, the Tide swept Marion Institute 10-0, 2-0, and 4-0.

One week after the history-making weekend against the Delta Devils, the baseball team managed another really big deal. In a 3-0 win over Kentucky in the SEC opener, the Tide pulled off the program's first triple play in fifteen years.

Like triple plays and no-hitters in baseball, "big deals" are important components of the unfolding of our lives. Our wedding, childbirth, a new job, a new house, key Alabama games, even a new car. In many ways, what we regard as a big deal is what shapes not only our lives but our character.

One of the most unfathomable anomalies of faith in America today is that while many people profess to be die-hard Christians, they disdain involvement with a local church. As Paul tells us, however, the Church is a very big deal to God; it is at the heart of his redemptive work; it is a vital part of his eternal purposes.

The Church is no accident of history. It isn't true that Jesus died and all he wound up with for his troubles was the stinking Church. It is no consolation prize.

Rather, the Church is the primary instrument through which God's plan of cosmic and eternal salvation is worked out. And it doesn't get any bigger than that.

It means you're throwing the ball good from the mound.
— Bama head coach Mitch Gaspard on the series shutout

**To disdain church involvement is to assert
that God doesn't know what he's doing.**

KNOW-IT-ALLS

Read Matthew 13:10-17.

*"The knowledge of the secrets of the kingdom of heaven
has been given to you" (v. 11).*

Carson Tinker knew something shortly before the national title
game started: Alabama was going to beat Notre Dame.

Tinker was an invited walk-on as a snapper in 2008. After a
redshirt season, he was the backup to senior snapper Brian Sel-
man in 2009. Over the next three seasons, Tinker was about as
bedrock solid as a snapper could be, considering the precarious
nature of the specialty. He started 40 games, handling all the long
snaps on punts and the shorter snaps on field goals and extra
points. He nailed 390 of his 394 snaps.

Tinker was among those who suffered personal loss from the
tornado of April 27, 2011. Among the six students killed was his
girlfriend; he was seriously injured. During an *ESPN* show about
the tragedy, Tinker said a lot of people expected him "to have the
'poor me's' . . . but I don't. . . . I have a positive attitude. And every
day is a blessing. It's a gift from God."

Before the championship game against Notre Dame on Jan. 7,
2013, as was his habit, Tinker exchanged a few pleasantries with
his Irish counterparts. "Their specialists were in awe," he learned.
"Certainly not of me, but of our team. . . . They were thinking, like,
'Whoa, we're playing Alabama.'"

Some of the Irish players came up to him, wished him good

luck, and congratulated him on landing a spot in the Senior Bowl. "I had never heard that from anybody we were about to play," he said. "It was just different."

What did Tinker learn from his pre-game encounter? "We'd been there before and Notre Dame hadn't," he said. He knew right then that his team was going to destroy the Irish.

We can never know too much. We once thought our formal education ended when we entered the workplace, but now we have constant training sessions, conferences, and seminars to keep us current whether our expertise is in auto mechanics or medicine. Many areas require graduate degrees as we scramble to stay abreast of new discoveries and information. And still we never know it all.

Nowhere, however, is the paucity of our knowledge more stark than it is when we consider God. We will never know even a fraction of all there is to apprehend about the creator of the universe — with one important exception. God has revealed all we need to know about the kingdom of heaven to ensure our salvation. He has opened to us great and eternal secrets.

All we need to know about getting into Heaven is right there in the Bible. With God, ignorance is no excuse and knowledge is salvation.

You are not defined by your circumstances or adversity. You are defined by how you respond to them.
— Carson Tinker on what he learned from the 2011 tornado

When it comes to our salvation, we can know it all because God has revealed to us everything we need to know.

DAY 65

ON NO ACCOUNT

Read James 5:13-20.

"[C]onfess your sins to each other and pray for each other" (v. 16a).

Alabama football was in trouble. And then Bear Bryant stepped up and held himself accountable.

"We kind of lost something the last two years," Bryant said in 1971 from the inner sanctum of his office. What Alabama had lost, among other things, was games, five of them each season. The Tide lost to Vanderbilt in 1969 and lost three games by more than 21 points in 1970. Auburn beat them both seasons.

So who was responsible? Bryant made it clear, using a scalpel on himself. "I blame myself," he said. "I've done a lousy job lately."

But even before anybody — except perhaps Bryant — knew that Alabama football was about to collapse, he began reconstructing. He turned most of his duties as athletic director over to someone else. He turned recruiting over to his assistants, reserving for himself only the final approval.

The veteran coach also changed his philosophy about offensive linemen. He had always preferred smaller, quick guys up front. By 1972, he had about a dozen linemen on hand who weighed 230 pounds or more, including the legendary John Hannah (273 lbs.).

The biggest change of all came after spring practice in 1971. Bryant decided he couldn't succeed anymore with a drop-back passer. "We had a good one last year in Scott Hunter, a real pro-style thrower, and we couldn't win," he said. So he junked his pro-style offense in favor of this new thing called the wishbone.

After Bryant's personal accountability resulted in a bunch of changes, did it do any good? The record's quite clear on that. From 1971-75, the Tide was an incredible 54-6.

Christians are herd animals, like, say, gazelles. Like them, we thrive when we surround ourselves with others of our kind. The lone Christian is like the lone gazelle, easy pickings for a predator. In Christians' case, the predator is Satan.

God calls us, the professed followers of Jesus Christ, to the kind of accountability Bear Bryant exhibited in 1971. We are to hold each other accountable as good parents do their children, as God does to us. That means we call out our brothers and sisters in Christ when they sin; it is not "anything goes" for Christians.

That doesn't mean, however, that we condemn or judge. Rather, we support and encourage; we demonstrate true, gentle Christ-like love, compassion, and concern. Ignoring the shortcomings and failures of other believers — and our own — is not an act of love, but rather intentional abandonment.

Satan is out there, waiting to pick us off one by one. In mutual accountability lie the strength and the support that provide our greatest defense.

I got to a point where I just expected things to happen instead of making them happen.
— Bear Bryant holding himself accountable for two mediocre seasons

**Holding each other accountable takes courage,
but it is foremost an act of Christ-like love.**

DAY 66

PROVE IT!

Read Matthew 3.

"But John tried to deter him, saying, 'I need to be baptized by you, and do you come to me?'" (v. 14)

Blake Sims had a lot to prove. After all, the Alabama coaches didn't want him to play quarterback.

When Sims signed with the Tide, critics proclaimed he'd never play quarterback for Alabama. Early on, they appeared to be right. Sims bounced from safety to slot receiver to running back as the Tide coaches tried to figure out what to do with him. He was redshirted in 2010 and played five games at running back in 2011. Even after Sims worked his way back onto the quarterback depth chart, he sat behind A.J. McCarron for two seasons.

As a senior in 2014, though, he was finally going to get the chance to prove himself to all his detractors. And then along came Jake Coker, a transfer from Florida State. The job was his to lose.

Or for Sims to take, which is exactly what he did. All that time in Tuscaloosa through all the disappointments and the constant barrage of naysaying, Blake Sims kept on working. The results showed up during 2014's spring practice.

His teammates saw it. They realized early on who was winning the battle to be the team's starting quarterback. Alabama center Ryan Kelly called Sims "a competitor" who worked in the film room until he knew the offense "from a variety of positions." He compared Sims to McCarron, calling them both "selfless leaders."

The week of the 2014 season opener against West Virgina, Nick Saban named Sims the team's starting quarterback. Still, though, he had to prove himself on the field. He did, spectacularly.

In 2014, Sims threw for 3,487 yards and 28 touchdowns, breaking McCarron's school record for passing yards in a single season. He was the MVP of the SEC championship game.

Blake Sims finished at Alabama with nothing left to prove.

You, too, have to prove ourself over and over again in your life. To your teachers, to that guy you'd like to date, to your parents, to your bosses, to the loan officer. It's always the same question: "Am I good enough?" Practically everything we do in life is aimed at proving that we are.

And yet, when it comes down to the most crucial situation in our lives, the answer is always a decisive and resounding "No!" Are we good enough to measure up to God? To deserve our salvation? John the Baptist knew he wasn't, and he was not only Jesus' relative but God's hand-chosen prophet. If he wasn't good enough, what chance do we have?

The notion that only "good" people can be church members is a perversion of Jesus' entire ministry. Nobody is good enough — without Jesus. Everybody is good enough — with Jesus. That's not because of anything we have done for God, but because of what he has done for us. We have nothing to prove to God.

He has exceeded my expectations.
— *Quarterback guru Ken Mastrole on Blake Sims*

The bad news is we can't prove to God's satisfaction how good we are; the good news is that because of Jesus we don't have to.

LEFT BEHIND

Read Luke 18:18-30.

"No one who has left home or wife or brothers or parents or children for the sake of the kingdom of God will fail to receive many times as much in this age and, in the age to come, eternal life" (vv. 29-30).

When Stephanie Schleuder left the University of Alabama, she did not leave behind what she hoped or expected she would.

Fresh out of graduate school in 1974, Schleuder packed all her belongings in her car and drove from Minneapolis to Tuscaloosa. She had been named the first head coach of the brand new Alabama women's volleyball team.

A $50,000 scholarship fund provided by Joe Namath was the spark behind the school's commitment to women's athletics. "They had teams before, but this was the first time that they had actually had a women's athletic program," Schleuder recalled.

That first volleyball team in 1974 went 6-13, but Schleuder didn't have another losing season. In 1976 and '77, the squad was an incredible 57-6 and 57-5.

After the 1981 season, Schleuder got a job offer from the University of Minnesota. She hesitated because rumors were floating that Alabama was set to cut a women's sports team. She feared her departure would seal volleyball's fate.

So Schleuder went to the administration and told them she wouldn't take the job "if there's any chance volleyball will be the sport that's going to be dropped." She was told the program was so successful that it would remain after she left.

She took the job that would take her home and continued to recruit for the Tide before leaving. Only as she prepared to head north did she learn the volleyball program had indeed been cut.

Schleuder fought for her athletes in the wake of a decision she called "devastating." Before she left, she worked to retain scholarships for some players and helped others find new places to play.

At some time in your life, you have left loved ones, friends, and family behind. Your new job meant relocating, so you had to say goodbye to those neighbors who helped you raise your children. You left your family to go to school or into the service. To buy your new car, you traded in your beloved jalopy. The phases of your life are often measured by what you left behind.

The truth is that we are often careless about not just the things but the people we leave behind. We are perhaps equally careless about what we say we would never leave behind.

But consider this question: What in your life would you leave everything else for? What would you walk away from your home, your job, your family, your friends, or your wealth for?

As with so many of life's questions, the only truly correct answer is Jesus. He demands that level of commitment; if he asks it, you must be willing to leave everything else behind for him.

I didn't go quietly. It was a very tumultuous time.
— *Stephanie Schleuder on leaving Alabama*

Your commitment to Jesus should be so total that you are willing to leave behind whatever he asks of you, knowing that greater rewards lie ahead.

DAY 68

MAKE NO MISTAKE

Read Mark 14:66-72.

*"Then Peter remembered the word Jesus had spoken to
him: 'Before the rooster crows twice you will disown me
three times.' And he broke down and wept" (v. 72).*

Joe Paterno made a mistake: He allowed himself to be over-
ruled by his assistant coaches. The result was "one of the most
famous plays in college football history."

No. 1 Penn State and No. 2 Alabama met in the 1979 Sugar
Bowl for the national championship. Midway through the fourth
quarter, Alabama led 14-7, but Penn State drove to a first down at
the Tide 8-yard line and then gained two yards on first down. A
second-down pass went to the 1-yard line.

Senior linebacker Barry Krauss, UA's defensive captain, called
Double-X Pinch, a risky call. It meant sending every defender
crashing into the middle of the line to stop a run up the gut. Anything but that, and the play probably went for a touchdown.

It was the right call. Senior linebacker Rich Wingo stopped the
Penn State fullback inches from the goal line. Fourth down. Time
out. On the Bama sideline, defensive coordinator Ken Donahue
calls Double-X Pinch again. Across the way, Paterno wants his
quarterback to fake a run and throw to the tight end. His assistants persuade him to run up the middle again. It's a mistake.

All-American tackle Marty Lyons crashed into the Penn State
backfield, blowing up the play. Wingo took out the lead blocker,

forcing the running back to leap over the pile. Krauss met him face mask to face mask. The hit was so violent that Krauss busted a rivet in his helmet and was momentarily paralyzed. Murray Legg rushed in from his safety spot and finished off the play by pushing the back onto the ground inches short of the goal line.

Penn State had made a mistake; Alabama had not. The Tide had held and went on to win the game and the national title.

It's distressing but it's true: Like football teams and Simon Peter, we all make mistakes. Only one perfect man ever walked on this earth, and no one of us is he. Some mistakes are just dumb. Like locking yourself out of your car or falling into a swimming pool with your clothes on.

Other mistakes are more significant and carry with them the potential for devastation. Like heading down a path to addiction. Committing a crime. Walking out on a spouse and the children.

All these mistakes, however, from the momentarily annoying to the life-altering tragic, share one aspect: They can all be forgiven in Christ. Other folks may not forgive us; we may not even forgive ourselves. But God will forgive us when we call upon him in Jesus' name.

Thus, the twofold fatal mistake we can make is ignoring the fact that we will die one day and subsequently ignoring the fact that Jesus is the only way to shun Hell and enter Heaven. We absolutely must get this one right.

When you make a mistake, admit it, learn from it, and don't do it again.
— Bear Bryant

Only one mistake we make sends us to Hell
when we die: ignoring Jesus while we live.

MAKE NO MISTAKE 137

DAY 69

YOU DECIDE

Read Acts 16:22-34.

"[The jailer] asked, 'Sirs, what must I do to be saved?'
They replied, 'Believe in the Lord Jesus, and you will be
saved'" (vv. 30-31).

Derrick Henry had to decide if he would leave Alabama.

Henry, of course, is now part of Alabama legend and lore, the 2015 Heisman Trophy winner, the school's all-time career rusher, and the SEC record holder for yards rushing in a single season.

Once upon a time, though, before that sensational junior season unwound itself and concluded with the Tide's fourth national title in seven seasons, Henry came frightfully close to leaving Alabama. In mid-December 2013, those closest to him gathered for what amounted to a full-fledged intervention.

A five-star recruit, Henry had arrived in Tuscaloosa in the fall of 2013 with expectations of rushing for at least 1,500 yards. Instead, he found three running backs firmly entrenched ahead of him on the depth chart. He discovered he had to learn to read defenses, block, and catch passes. With just 28 carries during the season, his dream had "turned into a nightmare of self-doubt."

Henry reacted as just about any other dazed and confused freshman on his own for the first time in his life might have: He wanted to leave Tuscaloosa and go home. So his parents and his former coaches met to set him straight. They reminded him he had made a commitment and laid out the possible future for him

CRIMSON TIDE

at Alabama: starting in 2015 after T.J. Yeldon turned pro.

But when the meeting broke up, they knew Henry had not made a decision. So his mother called Nick Saban, who was totally surprised that their future star was so unhappy. He revealed that plans were already in the works to elevate Henry to the No. 2 spot on the depth chart for the Sugar Bowl against Oklahoma.

Against the Sooners, everything clicked. Henry gained 161 all-purpose yards and scored two touchdowns. That clinched the decision; he would stay. The rest is Crimson Tide history.

As with Derrick Henry, the decisions you have made along the way have shaped your life at every pivotal moment. Some decisions you made suddenly and carelessly; some you made carefully and deliberately; some were forced upon you. You may have discovered that some of those spur-of-the-moment decisions have turned out better than your carefully considered ones.

Of all your life's decisions, however, none is more important than one you cannot ignore: What have you done with Jesus? Even in his time, people chose to follow Jesus or to reject him, and nothing has changed. As it was with the Roman jailer, the decision must still be made and nobody can make it for you. Ignoring Jesus won't work either; that is, in fact, a decision, and neither he nor the consequences of your decision will go away.

Considered or spontaneously — how you arrive at a decision for Jesus doesn't matter; all that matters is that you get there.

One game can change your life.
— Derrick Henry on the Sugar Bowl that helped him make a decision

A decision for Jesus may be spontaneous or considered; what counts is that you make it.

DAY 70

PRECIOUS MEMORIES

Read 1 Thessalonians 3:6-13.

"Timothy . . . has brought good news about your faith and love. He has told us that you always have pleasant memories of us" (v. 6).

As do so many others, Kermit Kendrick remembers Derrick Thomas. His recollections, however, are personal.

Not often can a defensive back fondly remember giving up a touchdown pass. Kendrick does, though. In the 1988 game against Penn State, which the Tide won 8-3, Kendrick, an All-American that season, surrendered a touchdown. It was called back for holding. What happened after that is what Kendrick remembers, always with a smile.

As Kendrick somewhat disconsolately made his way back to the defensive huddle, Thomas came over and delivered some encouragement. "Don't worry," he said. "He won't have time to throw the ball deep anymore." Thomas wasn't joking; for the game, he had three sacks, nine quarterback hurries, and a safety.

One of the greatest players in Alabama and football history, Thomas died in 2000 from injuries suffered in a vehicle accident. Memories of him became especially poignant in 2014 when he was inducted into the College Football Hall of Fame. The honor included a ceremony during Alabama's game against Southern Miss on Sept. 13. (A 52-12 Tide victory.)

Kendrick also remembers a Thomas moment from the Ken-

CRIMSON TIDE

tucky game that season. Alabama was trailing midway through the second half. At one point, the Wildcat offense broke the huddle, and Thomas had a message for them. "We are Alabama," he barked across the line, "and we don't lose to Kentucky."

Alabama didn't, rallying to win 31-27.

Your whole life will one day be only a memory because — even though you may push the thought down into your mind's deepest recesses — you will die. With that knowledge in hand, you can control much about your inevitable funeral. You can, for instance, select a funeral home, purchase a cemetery plot, pick out your casket or a tasteful urn, designate those who will deliver your eulogy, and make other less important decisions about your send-off.

What you cannot control about your death, however, is how you will be remembered and whether your demise leaves a gaping hole in the lives of those with whom you shared your life or a pothole that's quickly paved over. What determines whether those nice words someone will say about you are heartfelt truth or pleasant fabrications? What determines whether the tears that fall at your death result from heartfelt grief or a sinus infection?

Love does. Just as Paul wrote, the love you give away during your life decides whether or not memories of you will be precious and pleasant.

If you needed him, you didn't have to ask. He would be there and do it.
— Kermit Kendrick, remembering Derrick Thomas

**How you will be remembered after you die
is largely determined by how much
and how deeply you love others now.**

THE FINISH LINE

Read 2 Timothy 4:1-8.

"I have fought the good fight, I have finished the race, I have kept the faith" (v. 7).

It was a good start," Greg McElroy said about his first-ever game as Alabama's starting quarterback. It was a good start indeed, primarily because it finished well.

The redshirt junior got the call on Sept. 5 against 7th-ranked Virginia Tech in the 2009 season opener. McElroy knew he was as prepared as he could be. "I've been getting ready for this moment basically my entire life," he said the week of the game.

A lot of time on the sideline helped get him ready. He spent two years in high school behind Chase Daniel, who went on to star at Missouri. He then stood on the Alabama sideline for three seasons, one as a redshirt and two behind John Parker Wilson. He didn't just watch disinterestedly; he played the games in his mind. "I've taken thousands of reps in my head," he said.

At halftime of the Tech game, though, "McElroy was a mess." Alabama trailed 17-16, and he had completed only 6 of 18 passes. As McElroy stalked around the locker room, legendary Alabama running back Shaun Alexander walked up to him and offered some advice. "Take it easy," he said. "It will come."

It did. In the second half, McElroy completed 9 of 12 passes for 136 yards. With 12:51 left and the Tide trailing by a point, McElroy "lofted a 48-yard rainbow" to wide receiver Marquise Maze. On the next play, sophomore running back Mark Ingram scored. The Tide never trailed again and won 34-24.

Finishing strong, McElroy completed 15 of 30 passes for 230 yards with one touchdown for the night. He was the last player to leave the field, jogging alone toward the tunnel that led to the Tide locker room. Before he disappeared, though, he waved his right index finger in the air toward the celebrating Tide fans.

Paul compares the faith life to a race. His point is not that we are to drive ourselves to the point of exhaustion as runners often do, but rather that the most important part of our faith journey is the finish line.

Our lives will end; each of us will cross that finish line in one way or another. One of sports' most inspiring sights is that of a runner who falls down but nevertheless gets back up and finishes the race. Our faith lives must be like that.

We will stumble and fall down, metaphorically at least. In the personal race each of us runs, we will be tested, we will face hardships, we will be scorned and ridiculed, we will be called upon to make sacrifices, we will see our testimony rejected.

But for the disciple of Jesus Christ, these are merely hurdles, not barriers. Our task is to keep the faith; we keep running. When it's all over and the race has been run, each of us is the final arbiter of whether we finish the race in glory or in defeat.

He paced around the locker room talking to himself: it's not how you start, it's how you finish.
— Writer Lars Anderson on Greg McElroy at halftime vs. Va. Tech

**We win the race that is our lives
by keeping the faith.**

DAY 72

FAITHFUL LIVES

Read Hebrews 11:1-12.

"Faith is the substance of things hoped for, the evidence of things not seen" (v. 1 NKJV).

Sylvester Croom did not want to play center at all — until Bear Bryant said he had faith in him.

All Croom ever wanted to be and all he expected to be at Alabama when he arrived in 1971 was a tight end. So how come he and three or four other players from different positions wound up being drilled on their stances and starts repeatedly at practices? "None of us knew what it was for," Croom recalled.

Eventually, though, he overheard one of the assistant coaches talking about what was going on. The Bear was looking for his next center. Croom remembered his high-school coach had said that at college players were moved to center when they couldn't play anywhere else. "I didn't want to play center," he said.

At Alabama, though, the center position was not a mundane position where the refuse was tossed. The Tide has a long history of All-American centers: Carey Cox, '39; Joe Domnanovich, '42; Vaughn Mancha, '45; Lee Roy Jordan, '62; Paul Crane '65. The current center, for whom Bryant was seeking a successor when he left, was Jim Krapf; he would be All-America in 1972. (Dwight Stephenson in 1979, Antoine Caldwell in 2008, and Barrett Jones in 2012 would later join that star-studded list.)

After Croom's sophomore season, Bryant called him into his

office. He told Croom he would move to center, and he discussed how important the position was to the team's wishbone offense,.

Croom had one question: "Do you think I can do this?" Bryant's answer was unequivocal: "Yes, I think you can be good at it." His coach's faith in him cinched the deal; Croom would play center.

As Bryant had predicted, he was good at it. In 1974, his senior season, Croom was All-America and a team captain. He won the Jacobs Blocking Trophy as the SEC's best blocker.

Your faith forms the heart and soul of what you are. Faith in people (such as Bear Bryant's faith in Sylvester Croom), things, ideologies, and concepts to a large extent determines how you spend your life. You believe in the Tide and your family, in the basic goodness of Americans, in freedom and liberty, and in abiding by the law. These beliefs make you the person you are.

This is all great stuff, of course, that makes for decent human beings and productive lives. None of it, however, is as important as what you believe about Jesus. To have faith in Jesus is to believe his message of hope and salvation as recorded in the Bible. True faith in Jesus, however, has an additional component; it must also include a personal commitment to him. In other words, you don't just believe in Jesus; you live for him.

Faith in Jesus does more than shape your life; it determines your eternity.

He thought I could do it. That motivated me to get it done.
— *Sylvester Croom on Bear Bryant's faith that he could play center*

Your belief system is the foundation upon which you build a life; faith in Jesus is the foundation for your eternal life.

DAY 73

WORRYWART

Read Matthew 6:25-34.

"Therefore I tell you, do not worry about your life, what you will eat or drink; or about your body, what you will wear" (v. 25a).

For the fan of the Crimson Tide, there was just no since worrying about the upcoming bowl game. Heck, Alabama didn't stand a chance against Miami anyway.

The 1993 Sugar Bowl certainly presented the Alabama coaches with a lot to worry about. As writer Ron Higgins put it, "[Gene] Stallings' team was treading in deep water." Employing a sophisticated passing game, the top-ranked Hurricanes had won 29 straight games.

On the other hand, "Alabama was almost an afterthought in the polls," not considered a national contender before the season began. Even late into the year, the Tide didn't receive any first-place votes. By season's end, though, Alabama had risen to No. 2 and had won 22 straight games.

The Canes were unimpressed, taunting and laughing at Alabama with a braggadocio that was unseemly and classless. They declared they were too good to lose to "a one-dimensional team."

Ultimately, it was the dimensions of the Hurricanes that gave the Tide coaches hope. Miami lived by the short pass, and Stallings was convinced the Canes could not run on his defense. Secondary coach Bill Oliver spent nearly a month perfecting a scheme to nullify Miami's primary offensive weapons.

The Hurricanes never knew what hit them. Quarterback Gino Torretta faced formations he had never seen before. Sometimes, the Tide put eleven men on the line of scrimmage, "a naked challenge to Torretta." Cornerback Tommy Johnson described the result by saying, "Torretta didn't know what was going on."

What happened was three interceptions, a 34-13 Alabama romp, and the Tide's twelfth national title. Nothing to worry about.

"Don't worry, be happy," Jesus admonishes, which is easy for him to say. He never had a mortgage payment to meet or had teenagers in the house. He was in perfect health, never had marital problems, and knew exactly what he wanted to do with his life.

The truth is we do worry. And in the process we lose sleep, the joy in our lives, and even our faith. To worry is to place ourselves in danger of destroying our health, our relationships with those we love, and even our relationship with God. No wonder Jesus said not to worry.

Being Jesus, he doesn't just offer us a sound bite; he gives us instructions for a worry-free life. We must serve God and not the gods of the world, we must trust God and not ourselves, and we must seek God's kingdom and his righteousness.

In other words, when we use our lives to take care of God's business, God uses his love and his power to take care of ours.

If you don't like to worry, why do it? It won't help your performance.
— Joe Namath

**Worrying is a clear sign that we are
about our own business rather than God's.**

DAY 74

THE ODD COUPLE

Read Philippians 2:19-24.

"[Y]ou know that Timothy has proved himself, because as a son with his father he has served with me in the work of the Gospel" (v. 22).

Barrett Jones and William Vlachos were the Tide's odd couple.

The two linemen were roommates on the road in 2011. Vlachos, a senior center who would make forty straight starts, and Jones, a junior left tackle at the time who would finish as one of the most decorated players in Bama history, were "polar opposites in a lot of ways." They frequently made fun of each other's interests and often quarreled over control of the remote. Away from football, Jones could be found playing the violin or lining up his next mission trip. Vlachos would likely as not spend the same time wearing camouflage and sitting in a deer stand.

On their way to becoming "the ultimate combination" on Alabama's offensive line, they became friends. Vlachos once admitted, though, that his first impression of Jones wasn't exactly a good one. Jones agreed. "William thought I was weird," Jones said. "I wasn't a huge fan," Vlachos said. "He probably wasn't a huge fan either, but the rest is history. I love his humor now."

Their differences showed up once on *ESPN*. Jones wore long pants with his shirt tucked in; Vlachos rocked shorts and an untucked shirt. "But my hair was brushed," Vlachos noted.

Their odd-couple chemistry continued on the football field. They came to know each other so well that one could nod and the other would know what to do. That simpatico arose from their similar philosophies. Vlachos explained it as "giving everything you've got every play and knowing exactly what you're doing all the time." And winning.

Odd couples show up all over the Bible. One of the oddest is the pairing of Paul and Timothy. The two differed in age; Timothy was younger. Their temperaments clashed; Paul was fiery and demonstrative while Timothy was apparently shy and reserved. They came from different backgrounds; Paul was Jewish by birth, of the tribe of Benjamin, while Timothy was of a mixed Jewish/Greek heritage.

And yet God put this odd couple together to spread the Gospel. Timothy became Paul's most trusted lieutenant, and they grew so close that Paul referred to Timothy as being like his son.

This odd couple is just another example of the often inexplicable ways God uses people to advance his kingdom. In our faith life, we should never shy away from someone just because they look different or talk different. That person who seems so odd to us may very well be the partner God pairs us with to work for Jesus in glorious ways we could not imagine — just as God did with Paul and Timothy.

By the way, to that other person, you are the odd one.

It's like Fred Flintstone and Barney Rubble reincarnated.
— ESPN's *Chris Low on Jones & Vlachos*

There is nothing odd about two people, no matter how different, pairing up to work for Jesus.

DAY 75

FOCAL POINT

Read Psalm 73.

*"You destroy all who are unfaithful to you. But as for me,
it is good to be near God" (vv. 27b, 28a).*

In a bizarre finish, Emma Talley had to wait nearly an hour to take the shot that would win her a national title. Despite the distraction, she never lost focus.

Talley is the greatest golfer in the history of the Alabama women's program. She cemented her Crimson Tide legacy in 2013 by becoming the first Alabama golfer to win the United States Women's Amateur. Still, the NCAA individual title eluded her.

In May 2015, the junior entered the final round of the NCAA tournament with a one-stroke lead. Starting on the back nine, she carded nine straight pars. Other golfers wouldn't go away, however, and at one point she fell a stroke behind.

She approached the final tee still clinging to that one-stroke lead. Her tee shot promptly hit a fairway bunker. Unfazed, Talley hit a seven-iron from the sand and nailed it. She left herself with an 8-foot putt for a birdie.

"It was as good [a shot] as I've ever seen," said Tide head coach Mic Potter. "Uphill and into the wind, and to be able to hit it that solid. . . . It was pretty impressive."

At this point, everything was cut and dried. If Talley made the putt, she was the NCAA champion. If she missed it, a sudden-death playoff lay ahead.

Then as Talley lined up her putt, horns and alarms shattered the bucolic silence of the course. Lightning had been spotted in the area. Eight feet away from the title, Talley had to turn away from her putt and sit around and wait for 52 minutes. "I came back out," she said, "and all the nerves hit me again."

They didn't hit her hard enough, though, to break the focus she had maintained during the stressful wait. She nailed the putt to become Alabama's first-ever NCAA champion.

Living by faith and not by sight is sometimes tough. We quite often find ourselves distracted by what is going on around us. Like the psalmist of old, we look around and see the wicked prosper while the godly suffer; we succumb to despair. If we can't beat 'em, then we may as well join 'em. So we lower our eyes and our vision away from God and turn our feet from the path of righteousness and truth. We lose focus; we lose sight of God.

We can easily regain that focus, however. We need only consider the ultimate fate of those whom we have momentarily envied and sought perhaps to emulate, those who scoff at God, reject Jesus, and cherish the world's trinkets. Their prosperity is fleeting; its permanence is, as the psalmist says, an illusion that God one day will sweep away.

On the other hand, we who keep our focus on God will be sustained by him in this world and will one day be gathered with him into glory.

God's blessed me with so much, and I just took it and ran with it.
— Emma Talley on winning the NCAA title

**Children of the world focus on earthly rewards;
children of God focus on heavenly rewards.**

DAY 76

GOOD LUCK

Read Acts 1:15-25.

*"Then they prayed, 'Lord, you know everyone's heart.
Show us which of these two you have chosen.' . . . Then
they cast lots" (vv. 24, 25a).*

One lucky play" run only because the sub couldn't call it in the huddle spurred the Tide to a big upset.

Quarterback/defensive back Bobby Jackson played for the Tide from 1956-58. He described his first two seasons as "unpleasant." The teams won a total of four games, and Jackson and his coach, J.B. Whitworth, didn't get along at all.

Everything changed, though, when Bear Bryant arrived in 1958. "Coach Bryant turned out to be very tough," Jackson said in something of an understatement. For Jackson, though, the 5-4-1 season of 1958 made everything he had undergone worthwhile.

The 1-2-1 team was a big underdog against Miss. State in Starkville on Oct. 25. "We weren't supposed to give them much of a game," Jackson recalled.

The game turned on what Jackson called "one lucky play." That it was called at all was rather bizarre. On a third down, Bryant sent Norbie Ronsonet, "this big ole end we had from Biloxi," into the game with the play call. The huddle turned strange when all Ronsonet could do, according to Jackson, "was start chattering. I couldn't understand the play he was trying to tell us to run. No one could understand him."

So Jackson called the "one lucky play." He told Ronsonet just to go downfield about 30 yards, make a break, and "I'll throw you the ball." The call was a reverse pass, a play the team had worked on successfully in practice.

It worked again. Jackson took the snap, headed right, and then stopped and reversed his field. Ronsonet hauled in his pass and scored. That one TD on a lucky play held up. Alabama won 9-7.

Ever think sometimes that other people have all the luck? Some guy wins a lottery while you can't get a raise of a few lousy bucks at work. The football takes a lucky bounce the other team's way and Bama loses a game. If you have any luck to speak of, it's bad.

To ascribe anything that happens in life to blind luck, however, is to believe that random chance controls everything, and that includes you. But here's the truth: Luck exists only as a makeshift explanation for something beyond our ken. Even when the apostles in effect flipped a coin to pick the new guy, they acknowledged that the lots merely revealed to them a decision God had already made.

It's true that we can't explain why some people skate merrily through life while others suffer in horrifying ways. We don't know why good things happen to bad people and vice versa. But none of it results from luck, unless, as the disciples did, you want to attribute that name to the force that does indeed control the universe; you know — the one more commonly called God.

That was probably the biggest play of the year for us.
— Bobby Jackson on the 'lucky' touchdown play that beat Miss. State

**A force does exist that is in charge of your life,
but it isn't luck; it's God.**

FOR THE FUN OF IT

Read Nehemiah 8:1-12.

"Do not grieve, for the joy of the Lord is your strength"
(v. 10c).

Anyone paying attention would have known Alabama was going to beat Texas for the 2009 national title. After all, the Tide players and coaches made it clear that their idea of fun on the trip was to win the game.

Alabama's deadly serious attitude about the 2010 Rose Bowl was reflected even in the way the team traveled to Pasadena. The squad eschewed the $1,000 stipend the NCAA allows each player for travel expenses. Instead, the Tide traveled as a team "to make sure everyone arrived together and stayed focused."

The pre-game practices weren't romps in the California sun either. Rather, they were "physical, back-to-basics affairs." For Alabama, the whole affair was a business trip, not a vacation or a reward for the undefeated regular season.

Head coach Nick Saban even refused to play along with the false front coaches usually erect as they endure the media circus surrounding a national championship game. After his team had spent time at Disneyland, the Tide boss was asked at the opening press conference if he was having fun. "Is this fun?" he responded. "You know what's fun for me is practice. I really enjoy practice."

He wasn't joking.

As it turned out, the Tide had a whole lot of fun in California once the game started. They took care of business in the first half and jumped out to a 24-6 lead at the break.

In the last half, Texas tried to put some fun back in the game. The Horns got close before the Tide scored twice late to win 37-21 and claim the national title. Let the fun begin!

A very erroneous stereotype of the Christian lifestyle has emerged, that of a dour, sour-faced person always on the prowl to sniff out fun and frivolity and shut it down. "Somewhere, sometime, somebody's having fun — and it's got to stop!" Many understand this to be the mandate that governs the Christian life.

But even the Puritans, from whom that American stereotype largely comes, had parties, wore bright colors, and allowed their children to play games.

God's attitude toward fun is clearly illustrated by Nehemiah's instructions to the Israelites after Ezra had read them God's commandments. They broke out into tears because they had failed God, but Nehemiah told them not to cry but to eat, drink, and be merry instead. Go have fun, believers! Celebrate God's goodness and forgiveness!

This is still our mandate today because a life spent in an awareness of God's presence is all about celebrating, rejoicing, and enjoying God's countless gifts, especially salvation in Jesus Christ. To live for Jesus is to truly know the fun in living.

We're going out to win a national championship, not to go out there and have fun and party.
— Defensive end Brandon Deaderick on the Rose Bowl trip

**What on God's wonderful Earth can be
more fun than living for Jesus?**

DAY 78

PLAYING HARDBALL

Read Luke 13:22-30.

"[M]any, I tell you, will try to enter and will not be able to" (v. 24b).

The players were battered, bruised, and exhausted; the head coach talked about how hard the game was. That's the way it is when you take on LSU.

"That was hard," Nick Saban told his wife, Terry, after a hug and a kiss. To find her, he had to weave among a throng of media folks, for this was after the 2014 LSU game. The fifth-ranked Tide had just won a bone-crushing 20-13 game in overtime over the 16th-ranked Tigers. Writer Edward Aschoff described the game as one in which "two sledgehammers . . . bashed each other brains in for nearly four hours."

A field goal gave LSU a 13-10 lead with 50 seconds left, but the Tide stormed downfield behind quarterback Blake Sims. His biggest plays were successive completions to Christion Jones for 22 yards and to DeAndrew White for 16 yards. That set up Adam Griffith's 27-yard field goal that sent the game into overtime.

Sims then tossed "a beautiful, back-shoulder touchdown pass" to White from the 6-yard line. LSU went four and out. Game over.

The players and the coaches "celebrated like children." They sprinted toward the Alabama band and jumped in each other's arms. Saban even smiled. After that, though, the reality of the game's physical demands set in. On the flight home, Sims looked around and saw a bunch of exhausted teammates.

The next day, linebacker Reggie Ragland said, "It was tough, but I got out of bed. . . . My body was sore and I was mentally drained." He headed at once for the hot tub. Senior offensive lineman Austin Shepherd declared he was "sore everywhere."

The bruises and the soreness were expected from such a hard, physical game. So were the tired smiles that came with the win.

Unlike winning a college football game, finding salvation is remarkably easy: admit that you are a sinner, believe that Jesus died for your sins, and confess your faith in Jesus as your savior. For all too many, though, finding salvation is remarkably hard.

Jesus said as much, calling the entrance to Heaven "a narrow door." Being a good person won't get us through, no matter how kind we are to our mamas, children, and dogs. Doing good deeds won't let us squeeze through. Just knowing who Jesus is and having a dusty Bible around the house won't let us gain entrance. Even being a regular churchgoer won't earn us a free pass.

Finding salvation is hard because it ultimately requires effort on our part. We have to follow Jesus, not just believe in him. Even Satan *believes* in Jesus. We must live, think, and act a certain way, primarily with love. We have to study God's word and determine to live as it tells us we should.

As always, Jesus was brutally honest: living for him isn't easy; it's a narrow way. Sadly, for many people, the way is just too hard.

Like [I] got hit by a Mack Truck.
— *Lineman Austin Shepherd on how he felt after the 2014 LSU game*

**For too many people, following Jesus sounds easy
but just isn't worth the effort.**

DAY 79

SIZE MATTERS

Read Luke 19:1-10.

"[Zacchaeus] wanted to see who Jesus was, but being a short man he could not, because of the crowd. So he ran ahead and climbed a sycamore-fig tree to see him" (vv. 3-4).

Eddie Lowe didn't have a problem with his size, but a lot of other folks sure did.

Standing only 5-8, Lowe didn't consider his height to be a disadvantage even though he played linebacker. His opinion was not one that was universally shared.

Lowe learned how recruiters viewed his size one day in high school when he was working out in the weight room. A coach from Kansas showed up and asked him, "Do you know Eddie Lowe?" When Lowe identified himself, the coach "looked at me with a look that said I was kidding him. I guess I looked taller on tape." Without another word, the coach left.

Everybody kept telling Lowe what he couldn't do especially when what he wanted to do was play football for Alabama as his older brother, Woodrow, had. But Alabama's recruiters, along with those from other major schools, declared flat out that he was too small to play for them.

When Lowe headed to Tennessee-Chattanooga to sign his scholarship, his high school coach told him to wear some plat-form shoes to make him look taller. He did.

Lowe started as a freshman in 1979, but he wasn't satisfied with his situation at the school. At year's end, he gave up his scholarship to walk on at Alabama. It was a risky move, but it paid off. Before the start of his junior season in 1981, Lowe received a scholarship. His final college game was also Bear Bryant's last game. The player considered too small to play for Alabama was voted by his teammates as a permanent team captain in 1982.

After the NFL said he was too small, Lowe went on to an all-star career in the Canadian Football League.

Bigger is better! Such is one of the most powerful mantras of our time. We expand our football stadiums. We augment our body parts. Hey, make that a triple cheeseburger and a large order of fries! My company is bigger than your company. Even our church buildings must be bigger to be better. About the only exception to our all-consuming drive for bigness is our waistlines.

But size obviously didn't matter to Jesus. After all, salvation came to the house of an evil tax collector who was so short he had to climb a tree to catch a glimpse of Jesus. Zacchaeus indeed had a big bank account; he was a big man in town even if his own people scorned him. But none of that – including Zacchaeus' height – mattered; Zacchaeus received salvation because of his repentance, which revealed itself in a changed life.

The same is true for us today. What matters is the size of the heart devoted to our Lord.

It motivated me that people thought I was too small to play.
— Eddie Lowe

Size matters to Jesus, but only the size of the heart of the one who would follow Him.

HEAVENBOUND

Read Revelation 21:1-7.

"Then I saw a new heaven and a new earth, for the first heaven and the first earth had passed away" (v. 1).

Alabama's Patrick Murphy has declared Rhoads Stadium on the Alabama campus where his team plays to be softball heaven.

The softball program's head coach since 1999 delivered his appellation at the first game of the 2012 super regional against Michigan. Things had changed quite a bit since the last time the women from the Great Lakes State had come to town.

That was in 1997. The Wolverines were coming off back-to-back appearances in the College World Series. Alabama was coming off — nothing. It was the program's first season, and there wasn't much about it that was heavenly.

The team didn't have a batting cage, let alone a home stadium. The equipment shed was the trunk of any available car. Murphy was in the first of his two seasons as a Tide assistant coach.

Michigan swept a doubleheader from the Tide on March 4, 1997, at Munny Sokol Park, a public field "five miles and a river from campus and roughly a million miles from softball relevance." "There were probably 50 people and three dogs in the outfield at that game," Murphy recalled. "You couldn't believe it."

Officially, 2,475 fans gathered at softball heaven for that 2012 regional encounter. In a measure of how far the program has come, the crowd wasn't considered a big one, perhaps because of the looming holiday weekend and the sultry weather. Alabama typically leads the nation in attendance.

The crowd was loud, though. "We knew coming in what an environment it is in Tuscaloosa," the Wolverines' head coach said. "And, boy, on that field, it is so loud. We had trouble talking to our kids at time."

On that day in that raucous atmosphere in that beautiful home stadium, Alabama won 4-1. Just heavenly.

All too often Christians make the mistake of regarding Heaven as an abstract concept simply because they can't really imagine what it's like. Kind of like trying to figure out what God looks like or what Jesus' voice sounds like. But Heaven is a real place, as substantive as that TV set you watch the Tide on, that lawn mower you use to cut the grass, or those jeans you wear to work.

The Bible doesn't tell us all that we'd like to know about the believer's ultimate destination perhaps because it's much more interested in teaching us how to get there than in describing the lay of the land for us. God's Word is clear, though, that Heaven is a better place than the one we occupy now.

So why can't we have Heaven here on Earth? The answer is simple. On Earth, man's will clashes with God's; the result more often than not is chaos, confusion, and tears. In Heaven, though, God's will is achieved absolutely. The result is Paradise.

Heaven is real. You better believe it.

Welcome to softball heaven.
— Patrick Murphy to the third-base umpire before the Michigan game

Heaven is a real place where —
unlike here on Earth — God's will is done.

DAY 81

DIVIDED LOYALTIES

Read Matthew 6:19-24.

"No one can serve two masters" (v. 24a).

Auburn recruited him so hard the league office had to step in, but Vaughn Mancha stayed loyal to Alabama.

Mancha was a true 60-minute man. From 1944-47, he started four seasons at center and middle linebacker for the Tide. As the team's long snapper, he was also in on every special teams play. In one of the two Sugar Bowls in which he participated, he played every snap. He was All-America in 1945 and was inducted into the College Football Hall of Fame in 1990. In 1992, he was named to Alabama's All-Century Team.

Mancha was 6 years old when another child shot him in his left eye with an arrow. The accident left him with blurred straight-ahead vision in the eye, but it didn't keep him from starring in high school.

He signed with Alabama in 1941, but Pearl Harbor changed his plans. None of the four primary services would take him, though, because of his vision problems. He wound up in the Merchant Marine, moved to California, and worked repairing destroyers.

While Mancha was on the West Coast, his loyalty to Alabama was tested for the first time. A coach from UCLA recruited him hard, but Mancha politely declined. "All I could think of was wanting to get back to Alabama," he said.

The Army finally inducted him in 1944 but placed him on hold.

So Mancha returned to Birmingham where — to his surprise — he found himself being recruited hot and heavy by Auburn. The Tigers' insistence ultimately angered Mancha so much that he filed an official protest with the SEC. The league commissioner listened to both sides and then asked Mancha where he wanted to play. He made his loyalty to Alabama quite clear. "If I'm going to play," he said, "I'm going to play at Alabama."

And so he did.

More than once, Vaughn Mancha had to decide exactly where his loyalty lay. You probably understand the stress that comes with divided loyalties. The Christian work ethic drives you to be successful. The world, however, often makes demands and presents images that conflict with your devotion to God: movies deride God; couples play musical beds in TV sitcoms; and TV dramas portray Christians as killers following God's orders.

It's Sunday morning and the office will be quiet or the golf course won't be crowded. What do you do when your heart and loyalties are pulled in two directions? Jesus knew of the struggle we face; that's why he spoke of not being able to serve "two masters," that we wind up serving one and despising the other. Put in terms of either serving God or despising God, the choice is stark and clear.

Your loyalty is to God — always.

Alabama's still in my heart.
— Vaughn Mancha, about 60 years after he last played for the Tide

God does not condemn us for being successful and enjoying popular culture, but our loyalty must lie first and foremost with him.

DIVIDED LOYALTIES 163

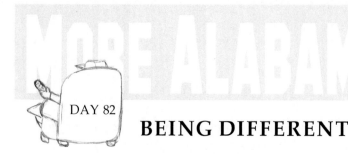
DAY 82

BEING DIFFERENT

Read Daniel 3.

*"We want you to know, O king, that we will not serve
your gods or worship the image of gold you have set up"
(v. 18).*

From his unique tattoos to his home country, Jesse Williams
was one different Crimson Tide football player.

Williams was a starter on the defensive line for the 2011 and
2012 national championship teams. He came to Alabama after
two seasons of junior college ball. That he won two national
titles in his only two seasons of major college football made him
different enough. But that was only the beginning.

First of all, there was his size and his strength. He was 6-foot-4
and weighed 320 pounds. That made him different enough, but
then he achieved legendary status in the Alabama weight room.
Before his senior season, he bench-pressed 600 pounds, "causing
a social media meltdown" when his feat was posted to his Twitter
account. Williams said he could have reached 640 pounds if the
coaches had been willing to let him try.

When he arrived in Tuscaloosa, he sported a mohawk, "causing
second glances and gasps" from innocent and amazed passersby.
But there was more. His body was covered with more than three
dozen tattoos. One was a poem his father wrote. Another read, "I
stopped checking for the monster under the bed when I realized
the monster was me." Another said, "Fear is a liar."

Williams' entire football career was one of a kind. He came to the game late, putting his first pads on when he was 15. Until then, he had played rugby and basketball — at home there in Brisbane, Australia, where he was born and raised. He is believed to be the first indigenous Australian to earn a college football scholarship in the United States.

Jesse Williams was and is just different.

While we live in a secular society that constantly pressures us to conform to its principles and values, we serve a risen Christ who calls us to be different. Therein lies the great conflict of the Christian life in contemporary America.

But how many of us really consider that even in our secular society we struggle to conform? We are all geeks in a sense. We can never truly conform because we were not created by God to live in such a sin-filled world in the first place. Thus, when Christ calls us to be different by following and espousing Christian beliefs, principles, and practices, he is summoning us to the lifestyle we were born for.

The most important step in being different for Jesus is realizing and admitting what we really are: We are children of God; we are Christians. Only secondarily are we citizens of a secular world. That world both scorns and disdains us for being different; Jesus both praises and loves us for it.

It was tough for some people to understand my Australian accent, so I tried to dull it down as much as I could.
— Jesse Williams on his different way of talking

The lifestyle Jesus calls us to is different from that of the world, but it is the way we were born to live.

DAY 83

A JOB TO DO

Read Luke 17:1-10.

"'We are unworthy servants; we have only done our duty'" (v. 10).

For Cornelius Bennett, game time was time to go to work.

From 1983-86 at Alabama, Bennett, a linebacker, was a three-time All-America. In 1986, he won the Lombardi Award as the best linebacker in college ball and was the SEC Player of the Year. He was named Alabama's Player of the Decade for the 1980s.

Bennett owed his success to the attitude he took toward playing football. For him, it was work. The hours weren't 9-to-5 but nevertheless, he had a job to do. "Every time I played, I just tried to do my job," he said. That outlook left him in the rather unusual position of never feeling any pressure, no matter how big or how pivotal the game was. He never felt he had to have a great game for Alabama to win; he just needed to do his job.

Bennett came by that approach quite naturally. He grew up watching his dad, Lino, who served in the U.S. Army and then worked for 33 years at U.S. Steel. "He was the hardest-working man who ever worked," Cornelius said. Folks who knew the senior Bennett described him as a quiet man who always went to work, no matter what. His son could not remember his dad ever missing a day of work.

"My daddy got paid every second Tuesday," Bennett recalled. "He'd come home on those Tuesdays and give me and my sister his paycheck to give to my mama." He never took any money out for himself before he delivered his check to the household. And so, Cornelius Bennett thought he should play football just the way his father worked.

Bennett never played for Bear Bryant, but he chose to "work" for Alabama in large part because of the Bear's TV show. "We always talked about him opening up that big bag of Golden Flake chips and drinking his Coca-Cola," Bennett remembered.

Like Cornelius Bennett for the Crimson Tide, we have a job to do for God. Back in high school or college when we did our work, we sometimes received extra credit. That same attitude has been known to bleed over into our faith life. If we visit a church member in the hospital or throw an extra $20 into the collection plate, do we feel like we have earned a little extra credit with God?

Jesus shoots that idea down by using the metaphor of a servant. The key to our job is obedience. If we follow Jesus Christ faithfully, then we are obedient to God. Everything we do for God should be an act of humble obedience, not one of self-serving pride. Obedience is our duty.

Even if we do our job and our duty totally and faithfully, we are still unworthy servants, Jesus said. Since we are just doing our job, the last thing we should expect is extra credit. What we can expect, however, is the reward we have been promised for our faithful service: Heaven.

I always thought I needed to do my job.
   — Cornelius Bennett on his approach to football games

**Each of us has a job to do for God: serve him
humbly, faithfully, obediently, and dutifully.**

DAY 84

EASY DOES IT

Read John 6:53-66.

"[M]any of his disciples said, 'This is a hard teaching. Who can accept it?' . . . From this time many of his disciples turned back and no longer followed him" (vv. 60, 66).

J.C. Wilhite's dream of starring for Alabama came true, but it sure wasn't easy.

Growing up in Tuscaloosa, Wilhite often rode his bike with his father to Sewell-Thomas Stadium to watch the Alabama baseball team. One day during that childhood, he declared that he would be a star on that field wearing the crimson and white.

Wilhite set 22 school records in high school. "We were very aware of him," said Tide head coach Mitch Gaspard. "We wanted him in our program and we liked him." The staff wanted others more than they did Wilhite, though; he didn't get an offer.

So Wilhite spent two seasons rolling up flashy statistics at a community college. When no offer of aid came from Alabama, he joined the Tide team in the fall of 2013 as a preferred walk-on.

He played in only eight games with two starts in 2013-14. He had only ten at-bats and struggled in the field at third base.

With only one season left to make his dream come true, Wilhite went to his head coach and asked what he could do to help the team. Gaspard had a rather strange idea. He had been looking for a sidearm pitcher and suggested that Wilhite give it a try. He did.

The kid who used to ride his bike to games wound up in the center of the 2014-15 team as one of the most versatile players in college ball. He started 51 of the team's 60 games and hit .307, third on the team. He also took the mound as a reliever eleven times with two saves and a 3.86 ERA. He was named to the watch list of the John Olerud Two-Way Player of the Year Award.

It wasn't easy but J. C. Wilhite's dream came true.

Making the starting lineup for the Crimson Tide is never easy, no matter what the sport. Neither is following Jesus.

It's not just the often abstruse aspects of Jesus' teachings that test us mentally. It's that Jesus demands disruption in our lives. To take even a hesitant, tentative step toward following Jesus is to take a gigantic stride toward changing our lives — and change is never easy. In fact, we abhor it; all too often we choose to live in misery and unhappiness because it's familiar. Something about the devil we know being safer than the angel we don't.

Jesus also demands commitment. We who live in a secular, me-first age are to surrender our lives to him. We are to think, act, live, and feel in a way totally counter to the prevailing philosophy of the world we temporarily call home. We are to keep our sights on the spiritual world and spend our lives in service and sacrifice now in exchange for a future eternal reward.

None of that is easy. But neither was dying on a cross.

A lot of it was self-determination and a will to get himself better.
— Mitch Gaspard on J.C. Wilhite's hard work

That which is easily accomplished in life
is rarely satisfying or rewarding;
this includes our following Jesus.

DAY 85

BLESS YOU

Read Romans 5:1-11.

"We also rejoice in our sufferings because we know that suffering produces perseverance; perseverance, character; and character, hope. And hope does not disappoint us" (vv. 3-5a).

Dont'a Hightower eventually came to see the most difficult time of his life as a blessing because it let him keep a promise.

A linebacker, Hightower was one of only two true freshman to start for the Tide in 2008. In the fourth game of the 2009 season, he suffered an awful injury to his left knee. Torn ligaments were just part of the damage. Hightower was done for what turned out to be a national championship season.

He worked hard to rehab his knee and returned in time for spring practice in 2010. He played the whole season, but he knew he wasn't the same athlete because of the lingering effects of the injury. "I couldn't do the things I wanted to," he said.

Thus, Hightower endured two seasons of frustration. Then, however, came 2011. A captain, he starred for the national champs and was an All-American. Since he hadn't played in 2009, the BCS title game meant "a lot more" to him.

But there was much more to 2011 than that. Had he not been injured, Hightower would probably have opted for the NFL after the 2010 season. In so doing he would have reneged on a promise. When he signed with Alabama, Hightower promised his grandfather that he would graduate. He did in December 2011 after taking 19 hours in the fall semester, a class load unheard of for a football player during the season.

His grandfather passed away before Hightower received his degree. Still, "I just set my mind to it, that I was going to go out there and finish the rest of my dream," he said.

He frequently recalled what his family told him. "My mom and everybody around me kept telling me that everything happens for a reason," he said. As Hightower came to see, that reason may have been that God had blessings stored up for him.

We just never know what God is up to. We can know, though, that he's always busy preparing blessings for us and that if we trust and obey him, he will pour out those blessings upon us.

Some of those blessings, however, come disguised as hardship and suffering as was the case with Dont'a Hightower. That's often true in our own lives, too, and it is only after we can look back upon what we have endured that we understand it as a blessing.

The key lies in trusting God, in realizing that God isn't out to destroy us but instead is interested only in doing good for us, even if that means allowing us to endure the consequences of a difficult lesson. God doesn't manage a candy store; more often, he relates to us as a stern but always loving father. If we truly love and trust God, no matter what our situation is now, he has blessings in store for us. This, above all, is our greatest hope.

God works in mysterious ways.
— Dont'a Hightower on the injury that became a blessing

Life's hardships are often transformed into blessings when we endure them trusting in God.

GOING OUT IN STYLE

Read Matthew 25:14-30.

*"Well done, good and faithful servant! . . . Come and
share your master's happiness!" (v. 21)*

Asked about repeating as national champs, Alabama's seniors
metaphorically shrugged their shoulders. But mention the legacy
they would leave behind — ah, that was something else.

Prior to the 2012 SEC Championship Game, the media and the
fan base were more than slightly bonkers at the notion of Alabama's repeating as college football's national champion. To the
team's nine seniors, two in a row was certainly nice; nicer still,
however, were three national titles in four seasons.

"Our goal was to accomplish something legendary that nobody
else has," said All-American senior center Barrett Jones. In other
words, the seniors wanted to go out in style, in a way no other
class in Alabama history had ever done. Indeed, not since Notre
Dame's national titles in 1946, 1947, and 1949 had any class won
three championships in four seasons.

"We know how small the window is," said senior linebacker
Nico Johnson. "[We] have to take advantage of this opportunity."

On Johnson's mind as it was the other seniors was the year
they didn't win the national title. The 2010 team was "probably
the most talented that [Nick] Saban has had at Alabama," but it
lost three games and wasn't part of the title discussion.

Experiencing that failure led the team's leaders to adopt a

particular mindset that let them wind up chasing history. It wasn't history they pursued each day but perfection, being the most dominant team on every play of every game of the season.

When the 2012 season ended the nine seniors — Jones, Johnson, safety Robert Lester, tight end Michael Williams, defensive end Damion Square, offensive guard Chance Warmack, deep snapper Carson Tinker, nose guard Jesse Williams, and defensive end Quinton Dial — had indeed gone out in style.

After they won the 2012 title, the nine moved on. While they had no choice, you probably have known times in your life when you felt it was necessary to move on, too. The job at which you had done all you could. The friendship that wasn't close any more. That tearful handing of your daughter to your new son-in-law. Sometimes you have no choice about the change, but you can always choose whether you exit with style and grace.

That holds true for life's end. We often picture "going out in style" to mean a fancy funeral with a long black hearse, a huge crowd, lots of flowers, and some famous preachers. At that point, though, you have long since departed this earthly existence. That expensive send-off is for those you left behind.

In sports, going out in style means finishing as a champion. When it comes to life and death, going out in style means only one thing: leaving with God's praise reverberating through your heavenly-bound soul: "Well done, good and faithful servant."

Don't go to your grave with a life unused.
— *Bobby Bowden*

**The only meaningful way to go out in style
is to leave this life with praise from God.**

THE LAST WORD

Read Luke 9:22-27.

"The Son of Man . . . must be killed and on the third day be raised to life. . . . [S]ome who are standing here will . . . see the kingdom of God" (vv. 22, 27).

Because an assistant coach had the last word, Alabama kept the quarterback who would become one of its greatest passers.

From Lake Butler, Fla., Andrew Zow was a top recruit until he tore his ACL making a tackle during a spring game in high school. He missed about half of his senior season. The injury drove many of his suitors away. The point was driven home when he attended a camp as a spectator and stood on the sideline next to Steve Spurrier, then the head coach at Florida. "He didn't say a word to me," Zow recalled. "That was really disappointing."

Alabama remained interested, however. He ultimately chose the Tide over Auburn because the Tigers wanted him to play linebacker. Alabama recruited him as a quarterback.

Almost as soon as Zow hit campus, the rumors started that he would be moved to defense. They were so rampant that he went so far as to pack his bags; he was ready to return home. But running backs coach Bruce Arians took him aside and delivered what amounted to the last word on the subject. "You are a quarterback," he told Zow. "Don't ever let them move you from this position."

With the matter settled, Zow unpacked his bags. He played during some up-and-down times, including the disastrous 2000 season. He spent much of his senior season in 2001 battling Tyler Watts for playing time. With the season in deep trouble, he was called upon to salvage it. He did.

The Tide was 3-5 when Zow took over. The last word about his career was a loud, successful one as he quarterbacked the team to four straight wins, including a bowl game. He finished up having set school records for career passing yards and career total yards (both records subsequently broken by A.J. McCarron, John Parker Wilson, and Brodie Croyle).

Why is it that we often come up with the last word — the perfect zinger — only long after the incident that called for a smart and pithy rejoinder is over? "Man, I shoulda said that! That woulda fixed his wagon!" But it's too late.

Nobody in history, though, could ever hope to match the man who had the greatest last word of them all: Jesus Christ. His enemies killed him and put him in a tomb, confident they were done with that nettlesome nuisance for good. Instead, they were unwitting participants in God's great plan of redemption, unintentionally giving the last word to Jesus. He has it still.

Jesus didn't go to that cross so he could die; he went to that cross so all those who follow him might live. Because of Jesus' own death on the cross, the final word for us is not our own death. Rather it is life, through our salvation in Jesus Christ.

I knew I was a quarterback and that I could play quarterback. I believed in my talent.
  — Andrew Zow, delivering the last word on where he would play

**With Jesus, the last word is always life
and never death.**

DAY 88

AT A LOSS

Read Philippians 3:1-9.

"I consider everything a loss compared to the surpassing greatness of knowing Christ Jesus my Lord, for whose sake I have lost all things" (v. 8).

The 1986 season opener tested not only whether the Tide could beat a good football team, but whether they could overcome a deep loss to do it.

On Aug. 27, 8th-ranked Alabama and 11th-ranked Ohio State met in the Kickoff Classic at Giants Stadium in New Jersey. Senior QB Mike Shula "ignored a busted blood vessel in his throwing hand [and] shrugged off a miserable three quarters of play" to lead the Tide on two late drives that pulled out a 16-10 win.

The game, however, was as much about what happened before the kickoff as it was the play on the field after the kickoff.

Sophomore defensive tackle Willie Ryles, who was scheduled to make his first start against the Buckeyes, had complained for several days to his roommate about headaches. On Monday, Aug. 18, he passed out during a half-speed, 9-on-7 drill. "I turned to ask him about the call he made, and he was lying on the ground like he was paralyzed on his left side," said noseguard Curt Jarvis. "At first I thought it was a stinger. . . . But then the stretcher came."

Ryles had a blood clot in his brain. He lapsed into a coma and never regained consciousness. Despite surgery, he died the Saturday before the season opener the following Wednesday.

Prior to the kickoff, the team gathered, and head coach Ray Perkins said a prayer for Ryles. Then on the day after the win, the team filed out of four chartered buses into a church in Columbus, Ga., for Ryles' funeral. He was eulogized as a gentle giant and a devout Christian. All-American linebacker Cornelius Bennett presented Ryles' mother with the Ohio State game ball.

"Buddy, you missed out," Jarvis told Shula when the quarterback said he had not known Ryles very well.

Maybe, as it was with the Crimson Tide in 1986, it was when a friend died. Perhaps it wasn't so staggeringly tragic: your puppy died, your best friend moved away, or an older sibling left home. Sometime in your youth or early adult life, though, you learned that loss is a part of life.

Loss inevitably diminishes your life, but loss and the grief that accompanies it are part of the price of loving. When you first encountered loss, you learned that you were virtually helpless to prevent it or escape it.

There is life after loss, though, because you have one sure place to turn. Jesus can share your pain and ease your suffering, but he doesn't stop there. Through the loss of his own life, he has transformed death — the ultimate loss — into the ultimate gain of eternal life. In Jesus lies the promise that one day loss itself will die.

I can't imagine what it would [be] like to lose and go to the funeral.
— Alabama guard Bill Condon at Willie Ryles' funeral

Jesus not only eases the pain of our losses
but transforms the loss caused by death
into the gain of eternal life.

DAY 89

DON'T FORGET

Read Psalm 103:1-5.

"Praise the Lord, O my soul, and forget not all his benefits" (v. 2).

Tony Nathan didn't forget. Even after thirty-six years.

Nathan was a running back at Alabama from 1975-78. He was second-team All-SEC in both '78 and '79 and was a team captain for the national championship team of 1978. He rushed for 1,997 yards, averaging a healthy 6.4 yards per carry. In 1999, he was inducted into the Alabama Sports Hall of Fame.

In the winter of 1979, his playing days at Alabama over, Nathan asked Bear Bryant for permission to drop some classes in his final semester. He had played in several all-star games and fallen behind; the professors had suggested he withdraw. Bryant agreed, but he exacted a promise: that Nathan would finish his degree.

Nathan promised. Maybe he meant it. He was 22 and a few months later he was drafted by the Dolphins in the third round. He went on and lived the life he had dreamed of. He married his high-school sweetheart and had an 8-year NFL career.

Mom and dad raised three daughters. They all graduated from college, two of them from Alabama. Then Nathan's wife completed her degree. "It's your turn," she told her husband. So he decided to honor his promise and take some classes.

Life got in the way once again. Nathan landed a series of jobs in the NFL. Finally, after the 2008 season, he left football behind for good. He became a bailiff in the courtroom of judge Ed Newman, a former Miami Dolphins teammate. And "Somewhere in there, I started to think of college again," he said.

On May 2, 2015, Nathan's long-shelved dream was realized. So was a promise he made a lifetime ago that he never forgot. Fifty-eight years old, he put on a cap and gown and received his college degree during Alabama's commencement ceremony.

While much about human nature is good — like not forgetting a promise made decades ago to an old coach long since dead — much about our nature is regrettable. That includes our rather distressing tendency to accentuate the negative in our lives while managing to forget all the benefits we have (think blessings).

Beyond the obvious such as food and shelter, what exactly is God doing at this moment in our lives that we should never forget? In his psalm, David says we start by not forgetting that God forgives our sins; he saves us. For believers, that means not forgetting Jesus Christ.

We should also never forget that God heals us, though often it's spiritual healing and not the physical healing we seek. We should never forget that God redeems us, transforming our lives and rescuing us from ourselves and from Satan. We should never forget that God fills our lives with his love and his compassion.

In short, we must never forget that God loves us so much he will do anything for us — even die.

I think they went to school when I played there.
— Tony Nathan on some of the professors he met at his commencement

When life is hard, we don't forget what God is doing for us, and we remember to praise him.

DAY 90

NO JOKE!

Read Romans 12:9-21.

"Do not be overcome by evil, but overcome evil with good" (v. 21).

When Alabama received an invitation to the 1926 Rose Bowl, folks across the country, including the media and coaches alike, thought the match-up was a joke. The joke was on them.

The widespread perception at the time was that Southern football was vastly inferior to that played by the powerhouses from other parts of the country. Wallace Wade's 1925 Alabama team, however, drew a lot of national publicity when it went 10-0 and surrendered only seven points all season.

The 10-0-1 Washington Huskies landed the West-Coast berth in the Rose Bowl. Officials then put out feelers to Dartmouth, Yale, and Colgate. They all declined in response to having recently come upon fire for putting too much emphasis on athletics.

Thus, in virtual desperation, the Rose Bowl looked South and officially invited Alabama. The reaction was immediate and predictable: The match-up was a side-slitting joke! A Seattle writer crowed that the Huskies would win by two touchdowns and "blow the Tide back across the continent as a pale pink stream." The legendary Pop Warner of Stanford declared Alabama to be "too light to stop that big Washington team."

When the Huskies led 12-0 at halftime, the West Coast fans began to politely applaud the Tide as if sympathizing with the overmatched Southerners. Then to their shock, Alabama scored three touchdowns in the third quarter, the first by quarterback Allison "Pooley" Hubert and the next two by halfback Johnny Mack Brown, who went on to a successful Hollywood film career. Washington scored late but fell short 20-19.

Southern football was a national joke no longer. Over the next 20 years, teams from the South played 13 times in the Rose Bowl.

Certainly the Bible is not a repository of side-splitting jokes, though some theologians have posited that Jesus' parables were actually sort of jokes for his time. Have you heard the one about the son who left his rich father and went to live with pigs?

No, the Gospel and its message of salvation and hope is serious stuff. Christians take it as such and well they should. Yet though many Christians might well vilify anyone who treats Jesus as a joke, those same persons themselves treat some aspects of Jesus' teachings as little more than gags not to be taken seriously.

Sexual purity, for instance. How outdated is that? And the idea of expecting answers to our prayers. What a silly notion! Surely Jesus was jesting when he spoke of tithing. How laughable is it to live performing selfless acts for others without getting the credit! And polls consistently reveal that about half of America's Christians don't believe in Hell. In other words, Jesus was joking.

No, he wasn't. If we think any of what Jesus taught us is a joke, then the joke's on us — and it's not very funny.

No one believed the Tide would be going.
— Writer Clyde Bolton on the 1926 Rose Bowl

Jesus wasn't joking; if we really love him, then we will live in the manner he prescribed for us.

DAY 91

JUST IMAGINE

Read Revelation 1:4-18.

"His face was like the sun shining in all its brilliance. When I saw him, I fell at his feet as though dead" (vv. 16b-17a).

Grant Hill never imagined he'd play football for Alabama.

The discus was the ticket that would pay for his college. In 2009, he set a Junior Olympic record for his age group. He won five national titles in the discus.

In 2009, Hill started on the line for his high school team as a freshman, but then his football career received a severe setback. He suffered from constant pain until in May 2010, doctors diagnosed the problem as a stress fracture in one of his vertebrae. The solution was a plaster cast that covered his entire torso.

He wore it from May to September, right through "the peak of Alabama's sweaty season." "They wouldn't let me do sprints. They wouldn't let me lift weights," Hill grumbled.

When the cast came off, he had gained about thirty pounds. Entering his sophomore year, he weighed a hefty 365 pounds. He set about losing some weight by cutting out snacks and drinking only water with an occasional Gatorade during workouts.

While Hill was slimming down, scouts came to Huntsville to look at a teammate. They came away impressed by the team's massive sophomore lineman. Word filtered back to Tuscaloosa.

In 2011, Hill and his family went to an Alabama game. They

met with Tide head coach Nick Saban, who did the unimaginable: He offered Hill a scholarship. The lineman's only condition was that he be allowed to throw the discus at Alabama. No problem.

Though he never imagined it, Hill saw action at tackle in five games as a freshman in 2013 and in seven games in 2014.

We are blessed (or cursed) with generally active imaginations. We can, for instance, quite often imagine what someone or some place looks like from a description. We probably have in our minds an image of what Jesus the man looked like.

Some things, however, are beyond our imagining until we experience them or see them in person. Bryant-Denny Stadium on game day. The birth of a child. Krispy Kreme donuts.

And add to that list the glorified Jesus. When Jesus ascended to Heaven, he assumed his rightful place in glory right there with God the Father, another unimaginable sight. In so doing, Jesus, the gentle man who drew children close to him and wept over the death of a friend, achieved a radiant splendor and glory the likes of which we can't really imagine despite John's inspired attempt to describe the scene for us.

Imagine this: One day we will see the glorified Jesus face to face. What we can't imagine is the depth of the joy that meeting will bring us.

I never imagined that I'd be playing Alabama football or going up against the best of the country.
— *Grant Hill*

The glorified Jesus is unimaginable as is the joy we will experience when we come into his presence.

HEART AND SOUL

Read Romans 12:1-2.

"Therefore, I urge you, brothers, in view of God's mercy, to offer your bodies as living sacrifices, holy and pleasing to God — this is your spiritual act of worship" (v. 1).

Ryan Iamurri told the Crimson Tide softball team and coaches she'd do anything to be a part of the program. She meant it.

During an unofficial visit to Tuscaloosa when she was a sophomore in high school, Iamurri sensed little interest. "Let's just say there wasn't a connection," she said. Coaches couldn't look past her height. She was 4-foot-10, not exactly the physical profile for a Division I program that annually competes for the national title.

So Iamurri spoke up. She told the assembled squad she would take on any role "up to and including that of water girl," to be a part of the program. She meant it, except perhaps for that part about the water girl.

Despite high school All-American honors and a .500 batting average one year, Iamurri's only full scholarship offer came from Jacksonville State. She was about a week away from taking the offer when, to her surprise, Alabama called. She wouldn't be a starter and would receive only limited financial assistance, but the coaches wanted her in the program and not as a water girl.

Iamurri's first season was 2011. Throughout her career, she was a role player, a singles hitter who specialized in pinch hitting. Her lowest batting average was .367 her freshman season.

Her career seemed to have ended abruptly and painfully her senior year during practice on March 12, 2014, when she collided with a teammate. She had a torn ACL. The only question she asked was if she could play through the injury.

Three weeks later, Iamurri stepped to the plate against South Carolina. Her teammates came out of the dugout, stood, and applauded her grit and determination to get back in uniform.

Ryan Iamurri was truly all in for the Crimson Tide.

When you stood in a church and recited your wedding vows, did you make a decision that you could walk away from when things got tough or did you make a lifelong commitment? Is your job just a way to get a paycheck, or are you committed to it?

Commitment seems almost a dirty word in our society these days, a synonym for chains, an antonym for freedom. Perhaps this is why so many people are afraid of Jesus: Jesus demands commitment. To speak of offering yourself as "a living sacrifice" is not to speak blithely of making a decision but of heart-body-mind-and-soul commitment.

But commitment actually means "purpose and meaning," especially when you're talking about your life. Commitment makes life worthwhile. Anyway, in insisting upon commitment, Jesus isn't asking anything from you that he hasn't already given to you himself. His commitment to you was so deep that he died for you.

I want to give every last bit of what I have to this team.
— *Ryan Iamurri*

**Rather than constraining you,
commitment to Jesus lends meaning to your life,
releasing you to move forward with purpose.**

DAY 93

ON OUR WAY

Read 1 Peter 2:4-12.

*"Dear friends, I urge you, as aliens and strangers
in the world, to abstain from sinful desires" (v. 11).*

Howard Schnellenberger hit the road with a clearly defined
mission: Don't come back to Alabama without Joe Namath.

It was 1961, and more than fifty schools had chased after the
gunslinger from Western Pennsylvania. Maryland won the lottery,
but Namath's SAT scores kept him out. The Bear swooped in.

He told Schnellenberger to take the trip north and bring the
prize to Tuscaloosa. The team's ends coach had known Namath's
brother from their playing days at Kentucky.

Schnellenberger left town with a fistful of $5s and $20s taken
out of a gunnysack of cash kept for just such emergencies. The
first time he saw Namath the kid was leaning against a wall in a
pool room in Beaver Falls. The coach's first impression was that
"he was 100% insolence."

Schnellenger had expected "to waltz in, charm some small-
town mill rat and catch the next prop out." It didn't turn out that
way. Instead, this "mill rat" was the "cock of the walk," wearing
a "one-button sports coat and baggy pants and twirling a chain."

For a week Namath escorted the coach around town and
generally yanked his chain. Schnellenberger had packed for three
days; his shirts "were moldering with wear." He had also run out
of money and was writing bad checks to pay his hotel room.

Finally, after a Sunday dinner of chicken and dumplings, the real person in charge decided to take charge. That was Namath's mother. She went upstairs, brought a bag down, and handed it to the coach. "Take him," she said. Schnellenberger did.

"Preferring a life of serial felonies to disappointing Bear Bryant even once," Schnellenberger wrote yet another bad check to buy the plane tickets for the return trip to Birmingham.

Few things changed the landscape of this country as did the construction of the interstate highway system. Chain restaurants, chain motels, entertainment districts in cities, the burgeoning of the trucking industry, from RVs to U-Haul trailers — we became a nation on wheels, a country of travelers. We fell deeply and irrevocably in love with the automobile.

As people of faith, we experience a wanderlust similar to that restlessness that drives us onto the open highway. Peter said we are "aliens and strangers in this world." That's because our true home, where we truly belong, is with God. We are just traveling through. Our ultimate destination is not Tuscaloosa, a nearby beach, or Walt Disney World; it is Heaven.

Believers in Christ all have dual citizenship. This precious little planet is truly just a way station for us. One day, each of us will make a final trip, the one to eternal glory, leaving all our baggage behind. Our traveling days will be over.

Go get him.
— *The Bear's instructions to Howard Schnellenberger* vis a vis *Namath*

**Some time today should be spent getting ready
for that one last trip you'll make,
the one to Heaven.**

DAY 94

A SACRED TRUST

Read 1 Timothy 1:1-14.

"Guard the good deposit that was entrusted to you —
guard it with the help of the Holy Spirit" (v. 14).

Every player who suits up at quarterback is the caretaker of a sacred trust." A.J. McCarron was so aware of how sacred that trust was that it once drove him to tears after a big win.

In writing of "a sacred trust," *ESPN's* Andy Staples spoke of Alabama and the legacy of quarterbacks such as Joe Namath, Ken Stabler, Pat Trammell, Jay Barker, Steve Sloan, and Harry Gilmer. The existence of that legacy makes quarterbacking Alabama's football team one of the toughest jobs in sports.

Barker knew it. He led Bama to a 35-2 record from 1991 through '94 and won a national title. "There is this intense pressure that your job is not to manage a game," he said. "Your job is to manage championships."

Just how much pressure that trust lays on Bama quarterbacks was illustrated after the game of Nov. 3, 2012, against 5th-ranked LSU. Alabama trailed 17-14 and had the ball at its own 28 with no timeouts and only 1:34 left in the game. McCarron led the offense on what was termed "a drive for the ages" to beat the Tigers 21-17. With 51 ticks on the clock, "the cool McCarron became legendary in Crimson Tide lore." He lofted a screen pass to freshman T.J. Yeldon, who went 28 yards for the game-winning touchdown.

As he hugged his parents after the game, McCarron's face

was littered with tears. Former Tide quarterback Brodie Cryole understood the emotion. "There was no show about that," he said. "Those tears were from the gut."

Such is the nature of the sacred trust at Alabama.

McCarron handled that trust perhaps better than anyone else ever has. He set the school record for wins (36) and is the only UA quarterback to win back-to-back national titles as a starter.

Christians know about sacred trusts because our precious faith is theoretically only one generation away from disappearing forever. In our hands and hearts, we hold the fate of a sacred trust that has been handed down across the generations for two thousand years. It comes to us not just consecrated by the blood of Jesus but also by the blood of martyrs, those who have died and are still dying today rather than surrender this sacred trust.

Every day, each one of us must decide what we are going to do with this trust. Will I ignore it? Will I let it sit idle? That is, will I do my part to let it slip one day closer toward extinction?

Or will I cherish it today? Will I guard it with all the love I can muster? Will I do my part to keep it alive by sharing it with someone today?

God has entrusted his kingdom to us until Jesus returns. What would we say to him if on that day, Jesus finds no one who claims his name? How would we explain away breaking God's heart?

In 2011, [A.J.] McCarron beat out Phillip Sims for the starting job and inherited that sacred trust.
— Andy Staples on how A.J. McCarron became keeper of the trust

We hold God's kingdom in trust
until Jesus returns to take over.

DAY 95

THE INTIMIDATOR

Read Luke 12:4-12.

"But he who disowns me before men will be disowned before the angels of God" (v. 9).

Hank Crisp may well be the most intimidating assistant coach Alabama has ever had.

Don Wade wrote, "Hustling Hank Crisp arguably made a larger impact on Alabama football than any assistant coach in the program's history." Crisp joined the Alabama staff in 1921, less than thirty years after the first season of Tide football. Incredibly, he was still coaching when Bear Bryant was hired.

In addition to coaching the line for the football team, Crisp served Alabama as athletic director, head basketball coach, head baseball coach, and head track coach. Alabama's indoor practice facility is named for him.

When he was 13, Crisp lost his right hand in a farming accident. That didn't stop him from playing football, basketball, and baseball and running track for Virginia Tech. A VMI coach once asked Crisp's coach why he didn't cut one hand off all his players.

The coach's signature statement, which drove fear deep into the heart of even the most stalwart player, was, "I've got a few little problems I'd like to work out with you." That meant dreaded one-on-one-time with Crisp.

Young Boozer, a halfback and a teammate of Bryant's, recalled that the coach had a leather kit that went over the nub of his right hand. "He could stick you [with that nub] every place you moved — stomach, chest, even in your face. [His inviting you out to practice] was the worst thing that could happen to you."

But the intimidating Crisp was also a soft touch for his boys. He once took a new pair of shoes off and gave them to a player. He also frequently handed his boys small amounts of money "he couldn't really afford to give away" when they needed it.

Intimidation is a major reason why all Christians don't answer the call God places on their lives, and every Christian does indeed have a calling from God. They sit timidly at church while some ministries wither. They pass meekly on the chance to witness to someone whom they know is an unbeliever.

To be intimidated is to be filled with and ruled by a spirit of fear, to be rendered timid. Others may intimidate us with an authoritative or brusque manner. Often, though, our intimidation comes from within; we talk ourselves into fear. It truly then becomes a spiritual problem.

Quite literally, that beer-swilling neighbor or that abrasive co-worker is dying to hear the Gospel. God places us in their paths. But they may well wind up condemned to Hell because we are too intimidated to speak up and tell them about Jesus.

Our Lord warned us against letting other people drive us to spiritual shyness and timidity. If we do, he said, then we will be disowned by God. *That* is what should intimidate us.

[Hank Crisp] put scars in my lip trying to teach me to be a linebacker.
— Fullback Tommy Lewis on his intimidating coach

**In being too intimidated to speak up for Jesus,
many Christians risk being disowned by God.**

NOTES
(by Devotion Day Number)

1   "I reached a point where I stopped believing,": Ron Higgins, "Transfer Worked Wonders for Donnelly, " *SEC Digital Network*, Nov. 30, 2012, http://www.secdigitalnetwork.com/SEC Nation/SECTraditions/tabid/1073/Article/239842/transfer.

1   His list of destinations . . . "You'll never play there.'": Higgins, "Transfer Worked."

1   "has been the gold standard for UA defenses ever since.": Chase Goodbread, "1992/2009: Donnelly vs. Green," *TideSports.com*, July 13, 2009, http://www.alabama.rivals.com/content/ asp?CID=958632.

1   "considered the best modern day unit in SEC history.": Higgins, "Transfer Worked."

1   Transferring to Alabama made me who I am.: Higgins, "Transfer Worked."

2   "was as good as anyone could ask him to be.": Pete Holby, "Auburn vs. Alabama 2012 Final Score," *SB Nation*, Nov. 24, 2012, http://www.sbnation.com/college-football/2012/11/24/ 3686780/alabama-auburn-2012-results.score.

2   "faultless in his decision-making.": Tommy Deas, "McCarron Pushes Right Buttons," *Tide Sports.com*, Nov. 24, 2012, http://www.alabama.rivals.com/content.asp?CID=1440884&PT= 4&PR=2.

2   McCarron spent the week . . . of the weakness.: Deas, "McCarron Pushes Right Buttons."

2   I felt like I . . . to do every play.: Deas, "McCarron Pushes Right Buttons."

3   Senior captain Scott Strohmeyer and . . . championship loss repeatedly.: Joe Menzer, "Sweet Redemption," *NCAA.com*, June 3, 2013, http://www.ncaa.com/news/golf-men/article/2013/06/ 02/sweet-redemption.

3   A few hours before play . . . was our chance, our opportunity,": Menzer, "Sweet Redemption."

3   The only Illinois point . . . national champions were gathered.: Menzer, "Sweet Redemption."

3   Not too many teams . . . two years in a row.: Menzer, "Sweet Redemption."

4   Mosley was not even listed . . . during the regular season.: Stewart Mandel, "Soft-Spoken Mosley the Key to Alabama's Vaunted Defense," *SI.com*, Jan. 6, 2013, http://www.sportsillustrated.cnn. com/college-football/news/20130106/cj-mosley-alabama.

4   the most important play of Alabama's national championship season.: Mandel, "Soft-Spoken Mosley the Key."

4   That he wasn't a . . . 20 percent of the time.: Mandel, "Soft-Spoken Mosley the Key."

4   At the team banquet, . . . to get out there,": Mandel, "Soft-Spoken Mosley the Key."

4   They asked me to . . . there and start mumbling.: Mandel, "Soft-Spoken Mosley the Key."

5   "It was during the time . . . player I've ever coached.": Ron Higgins, "A Man of Crimson Cloth," *SEC Digital Network*, Jan. 4, 2013, http://www.secdigitalnetwork.com/SECNation/SECTraditions/ tabid/1073/Article/240561.

5   Alabama gave me an . . . opportunity given to me.: Higgins, "A Man of Crimson Cloth."

6   "one of the titanic struggles of the college football season,": Kirk McNair, "LSU Wins Defensive Struggle in OT," *Tide Rolls* (Chicago: Triumph Books LLC, 2012), p. 94.

6   Cade Foster , the long-. . . lot of people behind me.": Andy Staples, "Alabama Kicker Jeremy Shelley Enjoys BCS Championship Redemption," *SI.com*, Jan. 10, 2012, http://www.sports illustrated.cnn.com/2012/writers/andy_staples/01/10/jeremy.shelley/index.html.

6   the kick was "nerve-racking . . . of this first game.": Staples, "Alabama Kicker Jeremy Shelley."

6   "Shelley, you're my hero, . . . "I love you.": Staples, Alabama Kicker Jeremy Shelley."

6   Lowest of lows, highest of highs.: Staples, Alabama Kicker Jeremy Shelley."

7   "Definitely on the defensive . . . will dribble or pass.": Don Kausler, Jr., "Tide's Ben Eblen Emerging as the Backup Who Doesn't Back Down," *AL.com*, Feb. 2, 2011, http://www.al.com/ sports/index/ssf/2011/02/tides_eblen_emerging_as_the_ba.html.

7   "I have a chance . . . hones on defense.": Kausler, "Tide's Ben Eblen Emerging."

7   We're driving to the . . . muscles [our guy] off.: source unidentifiable.

8   The Nittany Lions coach once . . . hurt the worst.: Ivan Maisel, "Matchup Sparks Memories of Bear," *ESPN.com*, Sept. 10, 2010, http://www.sports.espn.go.com/espn/print?id=5551302.

8   Jay Paterno, the coach's . . . going to kick your [backside].": Maisel, "Matchup Sparks Memories."

8   No bowl made a . . . what Alabama would do.: Maisel, "Matchup Sparks Memories."

9   "done with waiting, with . . . had won a championship,": Rick Bragg, "In the Nick of Time," *Sports Illustrated*, Aug. 27, 2007, http://www.si.com/college.football/2014/08/31/nick-saban-bear-bryant-alabama-crimson-tide-si-60.

9   "The comparison with Bryant . . . "came everything but locusts,": Bragg, "In the Nick of Time."

9   "the most storied, demanding and impatient program in college football?": Bragg, "In the Nick of

	Time."
9	There is never anything . . . can't live in it.: Bragg, "In the Nick of Time."
10	Offensive tackle D.J. Fluker said . . . out here and dominate." Tommy Ford and Mark Mayfield, *Crimson Domination* (Atlanta: Whitman Publishing LLC, 2013), p. 104.
10	In his halftime interview, . . . in the second half.: Ford and Mayfield, p. 99.
10	We came out, started . . . like we always preach.: Ford and Mayfield, p. 103.
11	Sington was so famous . . . became a national hit.: Richard Scott, *Legends of Alabama Football* (Champaign, Ill.: Sports Publishing L.L.C., 2004), p. 39.
11	Notre Dame coach Knute Rockne . . . greatest lineman in the country.": Scott, p. 41.
11	Against their rookie counterparts . . . "and a one-sided victory": Scott, p. 40.
11	"Let's try it.": Scott, p. 40.
12	assistant coach Alyson Habetz suggested . . . pulled it off at all.": Tommy Deas, "Morgan Is Undisputed Leader," *TideSports.com*, May 28, 2010, http://www.tidesports.com/apps/pbcs.dii/article?AID=/20100528.
12	I couldn't have asked for a better senior leader.: Deas, "Morgan Is Undisputed Leader."
13	Among his reasons was . . . young people, as I can.": Wayne Atcheson, *Faith of the Crimson Tide* (Grand Island, Neb.: Cross Training Publishing, 2000), p. 25.
13	Alexander once said that when . . .what kind of mood Chris is in.": Atcheson, *Faith of the Crimson Tide*, p. 23.
13	Alexander had a play in mind . . . and tight end Shawn Draper: Atcheson, *Faith of the Crimson Tide*, pp. 30-31.
13	Don't go down and we've got the game won.: Atcheson, *Faith of the Crimson Tide*, p. 30.
14	"about as bad a half of football as we've played all year.": "No. 1 Alabama Rides Cooper's 224 Yards, 3 TDs by Auburn," *SECsports.com*, Nov. 30, 2014, http://www.secsports.com/article/11951059/no-1-alabama-rides-cooper-224-yards-3-tds-auburn.
14	"to always be able . . . we certainly did today.": "No. 1 Alabama Rides Cooper's 224 Yards."
14	"the year of the flawed," . . . by the Iron Bowl.: Ivan Maisel, "Tide Proves They're a Perfect No. 1," *ESPN.com*, Nov. 30, 2014, http://www.espn.go.com/blog/sec/post/_/id/961604/tide-proves-theyre-a-perfect-no-1-in-a-season-with-no-dominant-team.
14	We misexecuted a lot of things,": Maisel, "Tide Proves They're a Perfect No. 1."
15	Hollingsworth was more interested . . . to meander through it.": William F. Reed, "'Bama Roars Back," *SI.com*, Oct. 30, 1989, http://www.si.com/vault/1989/10/30/120900/bama-roars-back.
15	Gary Hollingsworth continues to amaze me.: Reed, "'Bama Roars Back."
16	"To tell the truth, I had only planned to stay for one year," : Ralph Wiley, "How the Tide has Turned," *SI.com*, Feb. 2, 1987, http://www.si.com/vault/1987/02/02/114791/how-the-tide-has-turned.
16	recommended to athletic director . . . savvier, head coach at Alabama.: Wiley, "How the Tide Has Turned."
16	I was a no-name coach. I guess I still am.: Wiley, "How the Tide Has Turned."
17	Hightower grew up in . . . generation, two-way player,": Lars Anderson, "A Whole Lotta Everything," *SI.com*, Jan. 19, 2012, http://www.si.com/vault/2012/01/19/1061538/a-whole-lotta-every-thing.
17	Saban watched the junior . . . linebacker in the country.: Anderson, "A Whole Lotta Everything."
17	I knew right away he could be a perfect fit for what we wanted to do.: Anderson, "A Whole Lotta Everything."
18	His senior year in . . . "Is this good enough?": Austin Murphy, "Move Over, Gators," *SI.com*, Dec. 14, 2009, http://www.si.com/vault/2009/12/14/105886339/move-over-gators.
18	The Tide reduced "Tebow" . . . a lot to us.": Murphy, "Move Over, Gators."
18	Our standard was to be as good as Florida. Today we were better.: "SEC Championship Game: #2 Alabama 32 — #1 Florida 13," *Yea Alabama 2009* (Hanover, Mass.: Maple Street Press, 2010), p. 64.
19	the team had to fly . . . those old Aubuhn people.": John Underwood, "Bama's Big, Bold Bid in the Week That Was," *SI.com*, Nov. 23, 1964, http://www.si.com/vault/1964/11/23/614109/bamas-big-bold-bid-in-the-week-that-was.
19	A tackler in the . . . "Steve Sloan for President.": Underwood, "Bama's Big, Bold Bid."
20	McCarron came to Tuscaloosa . . . one he listens to,": L. Jon Wertheim, "Underrated," *SI.com*, Nov. 25, 2013, http://www.si.com/vault/2013/11/25/106400019/underrated.
20	Coming in as an . . . definitely — wasn't the wisest.: Wertheim, "Underrated."
21	Not until the fourth . . . of making some history.: Michael Casagrande, "The Inside Story of Alabama's Second Perfect Game," *AL.com*, Feb. 10, 2015, http://www.al.com/sports/index.ssf/2015/02/the_inside_story_of_alabamas_s.html.
21	"I looked at the . . . until it was over.: Casagrande, "The Inside Story."
21	"I kept the lineup card," . . . have it framed.": Casagrande, "The Inside Story."

193

21 It was one of those . . . about it, it gets jinxed.: Casagrande, "The Inside Story."

22 "While other players are . . . struggled to finish one.": Andy Staples, "The Perfectionist," *Sports Illustrated*, April 20, 2015, p. 75.

22 His mother, Michelle Greene, . . . all about that night,: Staples, "The Perfectionist."

22 I'm still kind of feeding off of that.: Staples, "The Perfectionist."

23 In the photo and in Moore's . . . to the ball carrier.: Tom Arenbereg, "The Other Tackler," *AL.com*, Sept. 8, 2010, http://www.al.com/sports/index.ssf/2010/09/the_other_tackler_barry_krauss_html.

23 In the first game of . . . into proving his coach wrong.: Arenberg, "The Other Tackler."

23 I made my share of mistakes — over and over again.: Arenberg, "The Other Tackler."

24 "It was brutal." Don Wade, *Always Alabama* (New York City: Simon & Schuster, 2006), p. 136.

24 there were no water breaks. . . . sweat out of his jersey.: Wade, *Always Alabama*, p. 138.

24 Bryant saw the rising . . . your fanny back down there.": Wade, *Always Alabama*, p. 137.

24 When Allen suffered a . . . to be in that hospital.": Wade, *Always Alabama*, p. 138.

24 The big guy couldn't get me in there.: Wade, *Always Alabama*, p. 139.

25 Men's coach Jay Seawall said he was . . . just a scraggly stray.": Caroline Gazzara, "A Tabby Cat in the Caddy Shack," *The Crimson White*, Feb. 23, 2015, http://www.cw.ua.edu/article/2015/02/a-tabby-cat-in-the-caddy-shack.

25 Her main job was to . . scampered through the golf complex.: Gazzara, "A Tabby Cat."

25 She would often steal . . . distracted by her antics.: Gazzara, "A Tabby Cat."

25 Seawall said she would sit . . . a bad run for a cat.": Caroline Gazzara, "Jerry the Cat Passes Away after Illness," *The Crimson White*, April 14, 2015, http://www.cw.ua/edu/article/2015/04/jerry-the-cat-passes-away-after-illness.

25 She's kind of a mascot, a very viable part of what Alabama golf is.: Gazzara, "A Tabby Cat."

26 In the stands, his parents . . . "We're gonna get it done,": Wade, *Always Alabama*, p. 224.

26 I had a little smirk on my face.: Wade, *Always Alabama*, p. 224.

27 the coaches put him on . . . "my whole outlook changed.": Tommy Hicks, *Game of My Life: Alabama* (Champaign, Ill.: Sports Publishing L.L.C., 2006), p. 100.

27 He understood that Bryant saw his . . . started at that meeting.": Hicks, *Game of My Life: Alabama*, pp. 100-101.

27 I figured [Bear Bryant] knew . . . back to the team: Hicks, *Game of My Life: Alabama*, p. 100.

28 In 1992, Simpson was a . . . all season long.": Corky Simpson, "Blue Collar to Blue Chip," Yea *Alabama 2009* (Hanover, Mass.: Maple Street Press LLC, 2010), p. 81.

28 Simpson remained anonymous . . . after week for Alabama.": Simpson, p. 82.

28 Not only did Simpson endure razzing from his fellow sportswriters but he received a lot of "unhappy, even hateful mail.": Simpson, 81.

28 Sports talk shows from all . . . questioned his knowledge of the game.: Simpson, p. 82.

28 I never doubted that the Crimson Tide was the best team in the country.: Simpson, p. 82.

29 "SEC coaches fell over themselves chasing after" Ragland: Alex Scarborough, "Reggie Ragland Finds Confidence," *ESPN.com*, Oct. 21, 2014, http://www.espn.go.com/blog/sec/post/_/id/91423/reggie-ragland-finds-confidence-emerges-on-alabamas-defense.

29 He "didn't look like . . . thick as tree trunks.": Scarborough, "Reggie Ragland Finds Confidence."

29 a starting linebacker spot was being handed to him.: Scarborough, "Reggie Ragland Finds Confidence."

29 He wondered if he . . . had in high school.: Scarborough, "Reggie Ragland Finds Confidence."

29 a starting linebacker spot was being handed to him.: Scarborough, "Reggie Ragland Finds Confidence."

29 Ragland turned to Collins . . . game and just ball.": Scarborough, "Reggie Ragland Finds Confidence."

29 Saban said that as . . . got better and better.: Scarborough, "Reggie Ragland Finds Confidence."

29 Because I hadn't played . . . everything was faster.: Scarborough, "Reggie Ragland Finds Confidence."

30 "The Crimson Tide didn't want . . . just wanted to play.": Graham Hays, "Alabama's Title a Milestone for SEC," *espnW*, June 7, 2012, http://espn.go.com/college-sports/softball/story/_/id/8017675/2012-womens-college-world-series-alabama.

30 Alabama "looked helpless": Hays, "Alabama's Title a Milestone."

30 By this time, it was . . . all the momentum.: Hays, "Alabama's Title a Milestone."

30 Alabama waited a long . . . in Oklahoma City.: Hays, "Alabama's Title a Milestone."

31 "Our offense is not . . . back at his ranch soon.": Douglass S. Looney, "Unbeaten and Un-Tide," *SI.com*, Oct. 10, 1994, http://www.si.com/vault/1994/10/10/132193/unbeaten-and-un-tide.

31 "the most unsatisfying 4-0 . . . disdain and suspicion.": Looney, "Unbeaten and Un-Tide."

31 "routinely unimpressive" Tulane: Looney, "Unbeaten and Un-Tide."

31   "Winning ugly is . . . making everybody cranky.": Looney, "Unbeaten and Un-Tide."

31   For some reason, I've gotten awful stupid lately.: Looney, "Unbeaten and Un-Tide."

32   As a youngster, Shultz . . . out of the way.: Hicks, *Game of My Life: Alabama*, p. 181.

32   His family moved while . . . was about six inches,": Hicks, *Game of My Life: Alabama*, p. 182.

32   "We'd like to offer . . . I want everyone to know.: Hicks, *Game of My Life: Alabama*, p. 184.

32   When injuries decimated the . . . he started on Saturday.: Hicks, *Game of My Life: Alabama*, p. 185.

32   I didn't think I was good enough to play at Alabama.: Hicks, *Game of My Life: Alabama*, p. 184.

33   "In my mind," he said, . . . That's a long time.": Ford and Mayfield, p. 147.

33   Square called his time at Alabama "something special.": Ford and Mayfield, p. 147.

33   He declared he could not have had a better college experience.: Ford and Mayfield, p. 148.

33   [Damion Square] came when . . . a great commitment.: Ford and Mayfield, p. 147.

34   "I literally grew up in . . . visit on her list: to Alabama.: Sean Landry, "Alabama's Dana Duckworth Living the Dream," *Tuscaloosa News*, April 16, 2015, http://www.tuscaloosanews.com/article/20150416/NEWS/150419646?p=1&tc=pg.

34   'Mom, I want to go . . . you have more visits': Landry, "Alabama's Dana Duckworth."

35   Cyrus once said that . . . wearing his football gear.: Alex Scarborough, "Kouandjio's Long Road to Alabama," *ESPN.com*, Nov. 29, 2013, http://www.espn.go.com/college-football/story/_/id/0051979/alabama-tackle-cyrus-kouandjio-took-long-route-cameroon-tuscaloosa.

35   "It's like a mentality," he said. "It was innate.": Scarborough, "Kouandjio's Long Road to Alabama."

35   the promise of a . . help his father out.: Scarborough, "Kouandjio's Long Road to Alabama."

35   What me and my brother . . . in your blood.: Scarborough, "Kouandjio's Long Road to Alabama."

36   In public the week of the . . . to light up after the win.: John Underwood, "Sorry, But Alabama Had to Run," *SI.com*, Oct. 29, 1973, http://www.sicom/vault/1973/10/29/618410/sorry-but-alabama-had-to-run.

36   Behind "a wedge of . . . eagerness to cooperate,": Underwood, "Sorry, But Alabama Had to Run."

36   Bryant was so impressed . . . bunch of con men.": Underwood, "Sorry, But Alabama Had to Run."

36   It was a five-minute burst of deadly reckoning.: Underwood, "Sorry, But Alabama Had to Run."

37   "waxing on about the . . . across the field.: Andrew Lawrence, "The Strong and Very Silent Type," *SI.com*, Jan. 19, 2012, http://www.si.com/vault/2012/01/19/106151259/the-strong-and-very-silent-type.

37   I'll say things when I have to.: Lawrence, "The Strong and Very Silent Type."

38   When newly hired head . . . broke down and cried.: Don Kausler, Jr., "More Than Anything, Mal Moore's Love Story Stands Out," *AL.com*, March 31, 2013, http://www.al.com/sports/index/_/ssf/2013/03/more_than_anything_mal_moores.html.

38   As the season moved . . . was diagnosed with Alzheimer's: Kausler, "More Than Anything."

38   I cannot put into words . . . over 50 years means to me.: Kausler, "More Than Anything."

39   those new designs "that . . . through traffic stops.": Alex Scarborough, "Arkansas a Blast From Past for Bama," *ESPN.com*, Oct. 15, 2013, http://www.espn.go.com/blog/colleges/alabama/post/_/id17256/arkansas-offense-a-blast-from-the-past-for-alabama.

39   "gone the way of the Dodo.": Scarborough, "Arkansas a Blast from Past for Bama."

39   Safety Vinnie Sunseri's immediate . . . around a little bit.": Scarborough, "Arkansas a Blast from Past for Alabama."

39   We pride ourselves on being a tough, relentless defense,": "No. 1 Alabama Silences Struggling Arkansas," *ESPN*, Oct. 20, 2013, http://www.scores.espn.go.com/ncf/recap?gameId=332920333.

39   There's comfort in the familiar returning from extinction.: Scarborough, "Arkansas a Blast from Past for Alabama."

40   given the school's proximity . . . not the coaching staff.": Joe Jares, "Alabama Stole the Show," *SI.com*, Oct. 17, 1977, http://www.si.com/vault/1977/10/17/622751/alabama-stole-the-show.

40   the Bear later admitted that he thought USC was "completely beaten.": Jares, "Alabama Stole the Show."

40   I have never seen a . . . quarter come back so strong.: Jares, "Alabama Stole the Show."

41   "That wasn't the most . . . and "Joshua 1:7.": Terry Mitrosilis, "Bama QB Beat UF While Honoring Auburn Student," *FOX Sports*, Sept. 23, 2014. http://www.foxsports.com/college-football/story/alabama-qb-blake-sims-honors-auburn-student-cancer-florida-game-cfb-am-092314.

41   "Kayla" was 19-year-old . . . together when it matters.": Mitrosilis, "Bama QB Beat UF."

41   Perry admitted that against . . . who was a friend.: Greg Ostendorf, "Alabama QB Puts Iron Bowl Rivalry Aside," *ESPN.com*, Sept. 22, 2014, http://www.espn.go.com/blg/sec/post/_/89172/sims-puts-iron-bowl-rivalry-aside-for-a-day.

41   We're really glad and thankful he did that.: Ostendorf, "Alabama QB Puts Iron Bowl Rivalry Aside."

42   When she made the . . . "It was so exciting.": Graham Hays, "Jackie Traina

Lifts Tide to WCWS," *ESPN.com*, May 28, 2011, http://www.espn.go.com/college-sports/blog/_/
name/college_sports/id?6602578/traina-lifts-alabama-crimson-tide-wcws.

42   [Jackie] Traina scored the . . . roaring their approval.: Hays, "Jackie Traina Lifts Tide to WCWS."

43   He pitched a no-hitter . . . sincere about football,": Wade, pp. 24-25.

43   "were tough, deliberate, painstakingly . . . quit practicing. It could.: Wade, p. 25.

43   I guess they were just scared to death of him.: Wade, p. 25.

44   "an "epic showdown": Alex Scarborough, "A Different Kind of Win for Alabama," *ESPN.com*,
Sept. 26, 2013, http://www.insider.espn.go.com/blog/colleges/alabama/post/_/id/16601/texas-am-
a-different-kind-of-win-for-alabama.

44   the game was "a shock . . . to expect from Alabama.": Scarborough, "A Different Kind of Win for
Alabama."

44   "Old-school Alabama turned . . . room broke into laughter.: Scarborough, "A Different Kind of
Win for Alabama."

44   You took ten years off my life. Scarborough, "A Different Kind of Win for Alabama."

45   The top ten list is found at *Sporting News*, "Top 10 Alabama Crimson Tide Players of All Time,"
http://www.sportingnews.com/photos/4634843-top-10-alabama-crimson-tide-players-of-all-time/
slide/299446.

45   Bryant once called him the . . . coached, regardless of position.: "Dwight Stephenson," *Wikipedia,
the free encyclopedia*, http://www.en.wikipedia.org/wiki/Dwight_Stephenson.

45   What makes guys like . . . to do those things.: Mark Inabinett, "Dwight Stephenson Mixes
Christian Testimony, Bear Bryant," *AL.com*, March 20, 2015, http://www.al.com/sports/index.ssf/
2015/03/dwight_stephenson_mixes_christ.html.

46   "My role wasn't to run . . . me to do, that's what I did.": Ford and Mayfield, p. 163.

46   Coming out of a smaller . . . and said, "What did I tell you?": Ford and Mayfield, p. 165.

46   He trotted out to begin . . . "I was playing tight end.": Ford and Mayfield, p. 163.

47   The trains were overloaded . . . to get to Pasadena.: Hicks, *Game of My Life: Alabama*, p. 5.

47   In the locker room, . . . got trampled in the rush.: Hicks, *Game of My Life: Alabama*, pp. 5-6.

47   It didn't matter. We . . . in the Rose Bowl.: Hicks, *Game of My Life: Alabama*, p. 5.

48   There was contact that . . . downcourt and wide open.: "Alabama Tops Georgia on Half-Court
Buzzer-Beater," *ESPN*, March 9, 2013, http://scores.espn.go.com/ncb/recap?gameId=330680333.

48   With two seconds on . . . and just long enough.": "Alabama Tops Georgia."

48   After Releford was swamped . . . practiced half-court shots.: "Alabama Tops Georgia."

48   I knew it was on . . . a little bit short.: "Alabama Tops Georgia."

49   In the game's closing seconds, . . . the coach's help with Namath.: Eli Gold, *Crimson Nation* (Nashville: Rutledge Hill Press, 2005), p. 127.

49   Werblin sent the Bear some . . . They were houndstooth.: Gold, *Crimson Nation*, pp. 127-28.

49   I offered him a Coca-Cola and he refused.: Gold, Crimson Nation, p. 127.

50   "I still think this . . . what happens up front.": Ivan Maisel, "Bama O-Line Bludgeons Notre
Dame," *ESPN.com*, Jan. 8, 2013, http://www.espn.go.com/college-football/bowl12/story/_/id/
8803941.

50   "the Notre Dame defense did its best imitation of butter.": Maisel, "Bama O-Line."

50   "a Hummer-sized hole created . . . left guard Chance Warmack.": Maisel, "Bama O-Line."

50   "stood there like a man waiting for a bus": Maisel, "Bama O-Line."

50   may be the best [bunch] . . . or ever been associated with.": Maisel, "Bama O-Line."

50   He called it. He just couldn't do anything about it.: Maisel, "Bama O-Line."

51   "We aren't going to . . . from start to finish.": Hank Hersch, "A New, Improved Tide," *SI.com*, Sept.
27, 1993, http://www.si.com/vault/1993/09/27/120358-a-new-improved-tide.

51   "How many times can you . . . improve as fast as Barker did.: Hersch, "A New, Improved Tide."

51   It was like going from tunnel vision to seeing everything.: Hersch, "A New Improved Tide."

52   Having previously narrowed his . . . and declared, "Roll, Tide!": Christopher Harris, "Landon
Collins' Mother Berates Son's Alabama Commitment," *bleacherreport.com*, Jan. 5, 2012, http://
www.bleacherreport.com/articles/1012761-landon-collins-mother-berates-sons-alabama-
commitment-on-live-tv.

52   Fifteen family members and . . . They applauded.: Alex Scarborough, "Landon Collins Eager
for the Next Chapter," *ESPN*, Aug. 25, 2014, http://espn.go.com/blog/sec/post/_/id/87143/collins-
eager-for-the-next-chapter.

52   From his mother, though, . . . of her son's decision: Harris, "Landon Collins' Mother."

52   going so far as . . . class and play hard.": Alex Scarborough, "Collins Looking Forward to LSU
Game," *ESPN.com*. Nov. 7, 2013, http://www.espn.go.com/college-football/story/_/id/99885301/
alabama-crimson-tide-landon-collins-remembers-hateful-reaction-commitment.

52   She knew Landon kept his promises: David Ching, "Landon Collins' Mom Might Require
Another Promise," *ESPN.com*, Dec. 30, 2014, http://www.espn.go.com/blog/sec/post/_/id/96232/

collins-mom-might-require-another-promise-from-son.

52 "Play hard or don't come home.": Scarborough, "Collins Looking Forward to LSU Game."

52 "I took a deep breath . . . even though I hated it,": Ching, "Landon Collins' Mom."

52 Landon Collins committed to . . . on national television.: Scarborough, "Landon Collins Eager for the Next Chapter."

53 She met her prospective . . . and four walk-ons.": Kayla Montgomery, "Mainz Mania," *The Crimson White*, Feb. 17, 2015, http://www.cw.ua.edu/article/2015/02/mainz-mania-ua-womens-tennis-coach-enters-nineteenth-season.

53 He called Mainz into his office . . . I'm going on a run.": Montgomery, "Mainz Mania."

53 The story behind the running . . . create in her locker room.: Montgomery, "Mainz Mania."

54 an "ideal showcase": Roy Blount, Jr., "It's Alabama in a Runaway," *SI.com*, Nov. 20, 1972, www.si.com/vault/1972/11/20/617964/its-alabama-in-a-runaway.

54 "too small for the . . . statistics [that] are ungodly.": Blount, "It's Alabama in a Runaway."

54 Bryant insisted that Davis could pass well enough.: Blount, "It's Alabama in a Runaway."

54 Davis "passed and ran . . . know what to expect.: Blount, "It's Alabama in a Runaway."

54 He passed so well . . . wishbone's running game.: Blount, "It's Alabama in a Runaway."

54 I don't know how . . . a regular season game.: Blount, "It's Alabama in a Runaway."

55 *Sports Illustrated* declared him to be . . . without looking at Bear Bryant.": Roy Terrell, "The Bear and Alabama Come Out on Top," *SI.com*, Dec. 11, 1961, http://www.si.com/vault/1961/12/11/621634/the-bear-and-alabama-come-out-on-top.

55 The powers that be were . . . from some wealthy boosters.: Terrell, "The Bear and Alabama."

55 For a man supposed to . . . people than anyone I know.: Terrell, "The Bear and Alabama."

56 He has quite gladly . . . players receive with them.: Michael Casagrande, "'Dinosaur Age': Alabama Unveils Its Brand of Hurry Up Offense," *AL.com*, Aug. 31, 2014, http://www.al.com/alabamafootball/index.ssf/2014/08/alabama_hunh_offense_saban.html.

56 With new offensive coordinator . . . Virginia's offense "fast ball,": Casagrande, "'Dinosaur Age.'"

56 It was something we hadn't . . . it helped us out a lot.: Casagrande, "'Dinosaur Age.'"

57 "the most fearsome unit in college football.": Lars Anderson, "Tide and Punishment,'" *SI.com*, Oct. 10, 2011, http://www.si.com/vault/2011/10/10/106117970/tide-and-punishment.

57 "there doesn't appear to be an offense in the land that can rally from a two-touchdown deficit": Anderson, "Tide and Punishment."

57 At this moment on a . . . thread of hope for [Florida].: Anderson, "Tide and Punishment."

58 Teeing off at No. 16, . . . tells me to do.": "Alabama Women Win First Golf Title," *ESPN.com*, May 25, 2012, http://www.espn.go.com/college-sports/story/_/id/793182/alabama-crimson-tide-women-edge-usc-trojans-win-division-golf-championship.

58 Her birdie putt from . . . "This is my moment,": "NATIONAL CHAMPIONS: Women's Golf Wins First NCAA Championship," *RollTide.com*, May 25, 2012, http://www.rolltide.com/sports/w-golf/recaps/052512aaa.html.

58 I can't think of . . . finish my senior year.: "NATIONAL CHAMPIONS," *RollTide.com*.

59 "a little piece of bottom . . . to make a living," Wade, *Always Alabama*, p. 45.

59 He often accompanied his . . . to turnips and watermelon.": Wade, *Always Alabama*, pp. 45-46.

59 during winter's coldest months . . . to quit after that,": Wade, *Always Alabama*, p. 46.

59 His father was a sickly man [and] the family was poor.: Wade, *Always Alabama*, p. 46.

60 "perhaps the most decorated player in Alabama football history.": Ford and Mayfield, p. 135.

60 "I want to be known . . . happens to be a Christian.": Ford and Mayfield, p. 135.

60 "My faith is not just another . . . It is my identity.": Ford and Mayfield, p. 137.

60 Late in the first quarter . . . miss a play at center.: Ford and Mayfield, p. 137.

60 he had to change his . . . I played all right,": Ford and Mayfield, p. 137.

60 I just didn't have much power in that foot.: Ford and Mayfield, p. 137.

61 "I'm just devastated,'" . . . complications from her diabetes.: Matt Hayes, "Alabama's Nico Johnson Carrying Heavy Burden into Title Game," *Sporting News*, Jan. 7, 2013, http://www.sportingnews.com/ncaa-football/story/2013-01-05/bcs-national-championship-alabama-vs-notre-dame-nico-johnson-uncle-died-mother.

61 One of the reasons he chose Alabama was so he could be close to her.: "Nico Johnson," *Wikipedia, the free encyclopedia*, http://en.wikipedia.org/wiki/Nico_Johnson.

61 "I was lost," he . . . everything including football.: Matt Hayes, "Alabama's Nico Johnson."

61 They were on his . . . to keep her son safe.: Matt Hayes, "Alabama's Nico Johnson."

61 Mamie raised him well. . . . never knew he had.: Matt Hayes, "Alabama's Nico Johnson."

62 With assistant coach Howard . . . your new quarterback,": Richard Hoffer, "Joe Namath the Qb and the Bear," *SI.com*, Jan. 17, 2013, http://www.si.com/vault/2013/01/17/106273078/joe-namath-the-qb-and-the-bear.

62 The assistant snorted in . . . before [his] eyes.: Hoffer, "Joe Namath the Qb."

63   "It means you're throwing the ball good from the mound.: Kevin Connell, "Alabama Makes History in Sweep of Delta Devils," *The Crimson White*, March 9, 2014, http://www.cw.ua.edu/article/2014/03/alabama-makes-history-in-sweep-of-delta-devils.

64   Among the six students . . . a gift from God": Ford and Mayfield, p. 153.

64   Before the 2013 championship . . . to destroy the Irish.: Ford and Mayfield, p. 151.

64   You are not defined . . . you respond to them.: Ford and Mayfield, p. 153.

65   "We kind of lost something the last two years,": Pat Putnam, "Pride in the Red Jersey," *SI.com*, Oct. 11, 1971, http://www.si.com/vault/1971/10/11/612456/pride-in-the-red-jersey.

65   using a scalpel on . . . thrower, and we couldn't win,": Putnam, "Pride in the Red Jersey."

65   I got to a point . . . of making them happen.: Putnam, "Pride in the Red Jersey."

66   When Sims signed with . . . to do with him.: David Albright, "The Making of Blake Sims," *ESPN.com*, Oct. 1, 2014, http://www.espn.go.com/college-football/story/_/id/11619467.

66   They realized early on . . . them both "selfless leaders.": Albright, "The Making of Blake Sims."

66   He has exceeded my expectations.: Albright, "The Making of Blake Sims."

67   Fresh out of graduate school . . . actually had a women's athletic program,": Kayla Montgomery, "Alabama Volleyball Team Set to Succeed," *The Crimson White*, Oct. 7, 2014, http://www.cw.ua.edu/article/2014/10/alabama-volleyball-team-set-to-succeed.

67   After the 1981 season, . . . new places to play.: Montgomery, "Alabama Volleyball Team Set."

67   I didn't go quietly. It was a very tumultuous time.: Montgomery, "Alabama Volleyball Team Set."

68   "one of the most famous plays in college football history.": "Barry Krauss," *Wikipedia, the free encyclopedia*, http://en.wikipedia.org/wiki/Barry_Krauss.

68   Senior linebacker Barry Krauss, UA's . . . a run up the gut.: Lars Anderson, "Stuff of Legend," *SI.com*, Jan. 13, 2010, http://www.si.com/vault/2010/01/13/105896576/stuff-of-legend.

68   On the Bama sideline, defensive . . . face mask to face mask.: Anderson, "Stuff of Legend.'

68   Krauss busted a rivet in his helmet: Arenberg, "The Other Tackler."

68   and was momentarily paralyzed . . . back onto the ground: Anderson, "Stuff of Legend."

69   In mid-December 2013, those . . . In the Sugar Bowl, everything clicked.: Alex Scarborough, "Derrick Henry's Decision to Stay at Alabama Paying Dividends, *ESPN.go.com*, Sept. 16, 2015, http://espn.go.com/college-football/story/_/id/13668573/alabama-crimson-tide-star-derrick-henry-thought-transferring-freshman.

69   One game can change your life.: Scarborough, "Derrick Henry's Decision to Stay."

70   As Kendrick somewhat disconsolately . . . the ball deep anymore.": Steve Irvine, "Remembering Derrick Thomas," *ROLLTIDE.com*, Sept. 12, 2014, http://www.rolltide.com/sports/m-footbl/spec-rel/091214aaa.html.

70   Alabama was trailing midway through . . . "and we don't lose to Kentucky.": Irvine, "Remembering Derrick Thomas."

70   If you needed him, . . . there and do it.: Irvine, "Remembering Derrick Thomas."

71   It was a good start,": Lars Anderson, "Thirty-Minute Delay," *SI.com*, Sept. 14, 2009, http://www.si.com/vault/2009/09/14/105855687/thirty-minute-delay.

71   "I've been getting ready . . . basically my entire life,": Anderson, "Thirty-Minute Delay."

71   "I've taken thousands of reps in my head,": Anderson, "Thirty-Minute Delay."

71   "McElroy was a mess.": Anderson, "Thirty-Minute Delay."

71   As the rookie quarterback . . . "It will come.": Anderson, "Thirty-Minute Delay."

71   "lofted a 48-yard rainbow": Anderson, "Thirty-Minute Delay."

71   McElroy was the last . . . the celebrating Tide fans.: Anderson, "Thirty-Minute Delay."

71   He paced around the . . . it's how you finish.: Anderson, "Thirty-Minute Delay."

72   All Croom wanted to be . . . didn't want to play center,": Wade, *Always Alabama*, p. 226.

72   After Croom's sophomore season, . . . be good at it." Wade, *Always Alabama*, p. 227.

72   He thought I could . . . me to get it done.: Wade, *Always Alabama*, p. 227.

73   "[Gene] Stallings' team was treading in deep water.": Ron Higgins, "Defense Lifts Alabama," *Memphis Commercial Appeal*, reprinted in *Sugar Bowl Classic: A History* by Marty Mule and found at allstatesugarbowl.org/site99.php.

73   "Alabama was almost an afterthought in the polls.: Higgins, "Defense Lifts Alabama."

73   They declared they were . . . the Tide coaches hope.: Higgins, "Defense Lifts Alabama."

73   Miami lived by the short pass: Austin Murphy, "The End of the Run," *SI.com*, Jan. 11, 1993, http://www.si.com/vault/1993/01/11/127874/the-end-of-the-run.

73   Stallings was convinced the Canes could not run on his defense.: Higgins, "Defense Lifts Alabama."

73   The Hurricanes never knew what hit them.: Higgins, "Defense Lifts Alabama."

73   Quarterback Gino Toretta faced . . . what was going on.": Murphy, "The End of the Run."

74   "were polar opposites on the . . . you're doing all the time.": Chris Low, "Tide's Jones, Vlachos

Always a Step Ahead," *ESPN.com*, Nov. 4, 2011, http://www.espn.go.com/blog/sec/post/_/id/32138/tides-jones-vlachos-always-a-step-ahead.

74 It's like Fred Flintstone and Barney Rubble reincarnated.: Low, "Tide's Jones, Vlachos."

75 "It was as good . . . It was pretty impressive.".": "National Champion: Emma Talley Wins," *RollTide. com*, May 25, 2015, http://www.rolltide.com/sports/w-golf/recaps/052515aaa.html.

75 Then as Talley lined up . . . nerves hit me again.": "National Champion: Emma Talley Wins."

75 God's blessed me with . . . and ran with it.: "National Champion: Emma Talley Wins."

76 He described his first two . . . didn't get along at all.: Hicks, *Game of My Life: Alabama*, p. 10.

76 "Coach Bryant turned out to be very tough,": Hicks, *Game of My Life: Alabama*, p. 13.

76 "We weren't supposed to give them much of a game,": Hicks, *Game of My Life: Alabama*, p. 14.

76 Jackson called "one lucky play." Hicks, *Game of My Life: Alabama*, p. 15.

76 On a third down, . . . successfully in practice.: Hicks, *Game of My Life: Alabama*, p. 14.

76 That was probably the biggest play of the year for us.: Hicks, *Game of My Life: Alabama*, p. 15.

77 Alabama's deadly serious attitude . . . back-to-basic affairs.": Todd Jones, "Title Wave," *Yea Alabama 2009* (Hanover, Mass.: Maple Street Press LLC, 2010, p. 7.

77 Head coach Nick Saban . . . I really enjoy practice.": Jones, "Title Wave," p. 7.

77 We're going out to . . . have fun and party.: Jones, "Title Wave," p. 7.

78 "That was hard," . . . throng of media folks,: Edward Aschoff, "Alabama Grinds Out Another Big Victory over LSU," *ESPN.com*, Nov. 9, 2014, http://www.espn.go.com/blog/sec/post/_/id/93120/alabama-grinds-out-another-big-victory-over-lsu.

78 "two sledgehammers . . . for nearly four hours.: Aschoff, "Alabama Grinds Out."

78 "a beautiful, back-shoulder touchdown pass": Aschoff, "Alabama Grinds Out."

78 The players and the . . . Saban even smiled.: Aschoff, "Alabama Grinds Out."

78 On the flight home, . . . "sore everywhere.": Alex Scarborough, "Alabama Turns the Page," *ESPN. com*, Nov. 11, 2014, http://www.espn.go.com/blog/sec/post/_/id/93290/alabama-turns-the-page.

78 Like [I] got hit by a Mack Truck.: Scarborough, "Alabama Turns the Page."

79 one day in high school . . . the coach left.: Hicks, *Game of My Life: Alabama*, p. 127.

79 When Lowe headed to . . . make him look taller.: Hicks, *Game of My Life: Alabama*, p. 128.

79 It motivated me that people thought I was too small to play.: Hicks, *Game of My Life: Alabama*, p. 131.

80 The softball program's head . . . regional against Michigan.: Graham Hays, "Alabama Wins at Speed of Sound," *espnW.com*, May 25, 2012, http://www.espn.go.com/college-sports/softball/story/_/id/7970604/ncaa-softball-tournament-alabama-crimson-tide-win-speed-sound.

80 The team didn't have a batting . . . the trunk of any available car.: Steve Kirk, "Tide Pride Showing," *The Birmingham News*, May 25, 2000, p. 01-D.

80 a public field "five . . . the sultry weather.: Hays, "Alabama Wins at Speed."

80 "We knew coming in . . . our kids at time.: Hays, "Alabama Wins at Speed."

80 Welcome to softball heaven.: Hays, "Alabama Wins at Speed."

81 In one of the two Sugar Bowls in which he participated, he played every snap.: Scott, p. 69.

81 Mancha was 6 years old . . . "I'm going to play at Alabama.": Scott, pp 70-71.

81 Alabama's still in my heart.: Scott, p. 73.

82 he achieved legendary status in . . . Another said, "Fear is a liar.": Ford and Mayfield, p. 159.

82 putting his first pads on . . . had played rugby and basketball: Ford and Mayfield, p. 160.

82 He is believed to be the . . . scholarship in the United States.: Ford and Mayfield, pp. 159-60.

82 It was tough for some people . . . down as much as I could.: Ford and Mayfield, p. 160.

83 "Every time I played, . . . to work no matter what.: Hicks, *Game of My Life: Alabama*, p. 165.

83 Cornelius could not remember the . . . football just the way his father worked.: Hicks, *Game of My Life: Alabama*, p. 166.

83 "We always talked about . . . drinking his Coca-Cola,": Hicks, *Game of My Life: Alabama*, p. 166.

83 I always thought I needed to do my job.: Hicks, *Game of My Life: Alabama*, p. 165.

84 Wilhite often rode his bike . . . program and we liked him.": Drew Champlin, "Alabama's J.C. Wilhite Living Out Childhood Dream," *AL.com*, April 2, 2015, http://www.alcom/sports/index.ssf/2015/04/jc_wilhite_alabama_dream.html.

84 Wilhite went to his head . . . Wilhite give it a try.: Champlin, "Alabama's J.C. Wilhite."

84 A lot of it was . . . to get himself better.: Champlin, "Alabama's J.C. Wilhite."

85 "I couldn't do the things I wanted to,": Chris Low, "Fate 'Smiles' on Tide's Hightower, Barron," *ESPN.com*, Jan. 5, 2012, http://www.espn.comblog/sec/post/_/id/36322/fate-smiles-on-tides-hightower-barron.

85 the BCS title game meant "a lot more" to him.: Low, "Fate 'Smiles.'"

85 When he signed with . . . happens for a reason,": Low, "Fate 'Smiles.'"

85 God works in mysterious ways.: Low, "Fate 'Smiles.'"

86 Asked about repeating as . . . that was something else.: Chris Low, "Alabama's Seniors Share Un-

breakable Bond," *ESPN.com*, Nov. 28, 2012, http://espn.go.com/blog/sec/post/_/id/56729/alabamas-seniors-share-unbreakable-bond.

86   "Our goal was to accomplish . . . that nobody else has,": Low, "Alabama's Seniors Share."

86   "We know how small . . . advantage of this opportunity.": Low, "Alabama's Seniors Share."

86   The 2010 team "was probably . . . every game of the season.: Low, "Alabama's Seniors Share."

86   Don't go to your grave with a life unused.: Jim & Julie S. Bettinger, *The Book of Bowden* (Nashville: Towle House Publishing, 2001), p. 76.

87   when he attended a camp . . . be moved to defense.: Hicks, *Game of My Life: Alabama*, p. 214.

87   They were so rampant . . . you from this position.": Hicks, *Game of My Life: Alabama*, p. 216.

87   I knew I was a . . . believed in my talent.: Hicks, *Game of My Life: Alabama*, p. 216.

88   "ignored a busted blood . . . three quarters of play": Hank Hersch, "The Tide Rolls with a Shula Named Mike," *SI.com*, Aug. 27, 1986, http://www.si.com/vault/1986/09/08/113921/the-tide-rolls.

88   Sophomore defensive tackle Willie Ryles . . . he had not known Ryles very well.: Hersch, "The Tide Rolls with a Shula Named Mike."

88   I can't imagine what it would [be] like to lose and go to the funeral.: Hersch, "The Tide Rolls with a Shula Named Mike."

89   In the winter of 1979, . . . Nathan promised.: Dave Hyde, "Former Dolphin Tony Nathan Keeps His Promise," *South Florida Sun-Sentinel*, May 7, 2015, http://www.sun-sentinel.com/sports/miam-dolphins/fl-hyde-dolphins-tony-nathan-0508-20150507-column.html.

89   "It's your turn," she told her husband. So he decided to honor his promise and take some classes.: Hyde, "Former Dolphin Tony Nathan."

89   "Somewhere in there, I started to think of college again,": Hyde, "Former Dolphin Tony Nathan."

89   I think they went to school when I played there.: Hyde, "Former Dolphin Tony Nathan."

90   Officials then put out . . . much emphasis on athletics.: Kelly Kazek, "The Original Mack Brown," *AL.com*, Dec. 26, 2013, http://www.al.com/living/index.ssf/2013/12/the_other_mack_brown_alabamas.html.

90   A Seattle writer crowed that . . . continent as a pale pink stream.": Clyde Bolton, *The Crimson Tide* (Huntsville: The Strode Publishers, 1972), p. 92.

90   Pop Warner of Stanford declared . . . to stop that big Washington team.": Kazek, "The Original Mack Brown."

90   When the Huskies jumped out . . . with the overmatched Southerners.: Bolton, p. 93.

90   No one believed the Tide would be going.: Bolton, p. 86.

91   He suffered from constant . . . the discus at Alabama.: Andy Staples, "Alabama Recruit Grant Hill Shines," *SI.com*, June 26, 2012, http://www.sportsillustrated.cnn.com/2012/writers/andy_staples/06/25/grant-hill-alabama-rivals-100/index.html.

91   I never imagined that . . . best of the country.: Staples, "Alabama Recruit Grant Hill Shines."

92   During an unofficial visit . . . and not as a water girl.: Graham Hays, "Ryan Iamurri Fights Back," *espnW.com*, April 8, 2014, http://www.espn.go.com/espnw/news-commentary/article/10748123/espnw-alabama-crimson-tide-pinch-hitter-ryan-iamurri-fights-way-back.

92   during practice on March . . . get back in uniform.: Hays, "Ryan Iamurri Fights Back."

92   I want to give every last bit of what I have to this team.: Hays, "Ryan Iamurri Fights Back."

93   more than fifty schools . . . plane tickets to Birmingham.: Hoffer, "Joe Namath the Qb and the Bear."

93   Go get him.: Hoffer, "Joe Namath the Qb and the Bear."

94   Every player who suits up . . . caretaker of a sacred trust." Andy Staples, "Rolling with the Tide," *SI.com*, Jan. 17, 2013, http://www.si.com/vault/2013/01/17/06273076-rolling-with-the-tide.

94   The existence of that . . . toughest jobs in sports.: Staples, "Rolling with the Tide."

94   "There is this intense pressure . . . to manage championships.: Staples, "Rolling with the Tide."

94   "a drive for the ages": Staples, "Rolling with the Tide."

94   "the cool McCarron became legendary in Crimson Tide lore.": Ford and Mayfield, p. 62.

94   As he hugged his . . . were from the gut.": Staples, "Rolling with the Tide."

94   In 2011, [A.J.] McCarron beat out Phillip Sims for the starting job and inherited that sacred trust.: Staples, "Rolling with the Tide."

95   "Hustling Hank Crisp made . . . in the program's history.": Wade, *Always Alabama*, p. 37.

95   When he was 13, . . . off all his players.: "Hank Crisp," *Wikipedia, the free encyclopedia*, http://en.wikipedia.org/wiki/Hank_Crisp.

95   The coach's signature statement . . . when they needed it.: Wade, *Always Alabama*, p. 37.

95   [Hank Crisp] put scars . . . to be a linebacker.: Wade, *Always Alabama*, p. 37.

WORKS CITED

"Alabama Tops Georgia on Half-Court Buzzer-Beater." *ESPN.com*. 9 March 2013. http://scores.espn.go.com/ncb/recap?gameId=330680333.

"Alabama Women Win First Golf Title." *ESPN.com*. 25 May 2012. http://www.espn.go.com/college-sports/story/_/id/7973182/alabama-crimson-tide-women-edge-usc-trojans-win-division-golf-championship.

Albright, David. "The Making of Blake Sims." *ESPN*. 1 Oct. 2014. http://www.espn.go.com/college-football/story/_/id/11619467.blake-sims-had-many-guiding-hands-road-becoming-alabama-crimson-tide-quarterback.

Anderson, Lars. "A Whole Lotta Everything." *SI.com*. 19 Jan. 2012. http://www.si.com/vault/2012/01/19/1061538/a-whole-lotta-everything.

-----. "Stuff of Legend." *SI.com*. 13 Jan. 2010. http://www.si.com/vault/2010/01/13/105896576/stuff-of-legend.

-----. "Thirty-Minute Delay." *SI.com*. 14 Sept. 2009. http://www.si.com/vault/2009/09/14/105855687/thirty-minute-delay.

-----. "Tide and Punishment." *SI.com*. 10 Oct. 2011. http://www.si.com/vault/2011/10/10/106117970/tide-and-punishment.

Arenberg, Tom. "The Other Tackler." *AL.com*. 8 Sept. 2010. http://www.al.com/sports/index.ssf/2010/09/the_other_tackler_barry_krauss_html.

Aschoff, Edward. "Alabama Grinds Out Another Big Victory over LSU." *ESPN.com*. 9 Nov. 2014. http://www.espn.go.com/blog/sec/post/_/id/93220/albama-grinds-out-another-big-victory-over-lsu.

-----. "Creativity Gets Alabama on the Board First." *ESPN.com*. 26 Nov. 2011. http://www.espn.go.com/blog/sec/post/_/id/33852/creativity-gets-alabama-on-the-board-first.

Atcheson, Wayne. *Faith of the Crimson Tide*. Grand Island, Neb.: Cross Training Publishing, 2000.

"Barry Krauss." *Wikipedia, the free encyclopedia*. http://en.wikipedia.org/wiki/Barry_Krauss.

Bettinger, Jim & Julie S. *The Book of Bowden*. Nashville: Towle House Publishing, 2001.

Blount, Roy, Jr. "It's Alabama in a Runaway." *SI.com*. 20 Nov. 1972. http://www.si.com/vault/1972/11/20/617964/its-alabama-in-a-runaway.

Bolton, Clyde. *The Crimson Tide: A Story of Alabama Football*. Huntsville: The Strode Publishers, 1972.

Bragg, Rick. "In the Nick of Time: Alabama's Faithful Welcome Their Savior." *Sports Illustrated*. 27 Aug. 2007, http://www.si.com/college-football/2014-08-31-nick-saban-bear-bryant-alabama-crimson-tide-si-60.

Casagrande, Michael. "'Dinosaur Age': Alabama Unveils Its Brand of Hurry Up Offense." *AL.com*. 31 Aug. 2014. http://www.al.com/alabamafootball/index.ssf.2014/08/alabama_huhn_offense_saban.html.

-----. "The Inside Story of Alabama's Second Perfect Game in Softball Program History." *AL.com*. 10 Feb. 2015. http://www.al.com/sports/index.ssf/2015/02/the_inside_story_of_alabamas_s.html.

Champlin, Drew. "Alabama's J.C. Wilhite Living Out Childhood Dream of Starring for Crimson Tide." *AL.com*. 2 April 2015. http://www.al.com/sports/index.ssf/2015/04/jc_wilhite_alabama_dream.html.

Ching, David. "Landon Collins' Mom Might Require Another Promise from Son." *ESPN.com*. 30 Dec. 2014. http://www.espn.go.com/blog/sec/post/_/id/96232/collins-mom-might-require-another-promise-from-son.

Connell, Kevin. "Alabama Makes History in Sweep of Delta Devils." *The Crimson White.* 3 March 2014. http://www.cw.ua.edu/article/2014/03/alabama-makes-history-in-sweep-of-delta-devils.

Deas, Tommy. "McCarron Pushes Right Buttons." *TideSports.com.* 24 Nov. 2012, http://www.alabama.rivals.com/content.asp?CID=1440884&PT=4&PR=2.

-----. "Morgan is Undisputed Leader." *TideSports.com.* 28 May 2010. http://www.tidesports.com/apps/pbcs.dll/article?AID=/20100528.

"Dwight Stephenson." *Wikipedia, the free encyclopedia.* http://www.en.wikipedia.org. wiki/Dwight_Stephenson.

Ford, Tommy and Mark Mayfield. *Crimson Domination: The Process Behind Alabama's 15th National Championship.* Atlanta: Whitman Publishing, LLC, 2013.

Gazzara. Caroline. "A Tabby Cat in the Caddy Shack: Jerry Serves as Unofficial Mascot for UA Golf Teams." *The Crimson White.* 23 Feb. 2015. http://www.cw.ua.edu/article/2015/02/a-tabby-cat-in-the-caddy-shack.

-----. "Jerry the Cat Passes Away after Illness." *The Crimson White.* 14 April 2015. http://www.cw.ua.edu/article/2015/04/jerry-the-cat-passes-away-after-illness.

Gold, Eli. *Crimson Nation.* Nashville: Rutledge Hill Press, 2005.

Goodbread, Chase. "1992/2009: Donnelly vs. Green." *TideSports.com.* 13 July 2009. http://www.alabamarivals.com/content/asp?CID=958632.

"Hank Crisp." *Wikipedia, the free encyclopedia.* http://en.wikipedia.org/wiki/Hank_Crisp.

Harris, Christopher. "Landon Collins' Mother Berates Son's Alabama Commitment on Live TV." *bleacherreport.com.* 5 Jan. 2012, http://www.bleacherreport.com/articles/1012761-landon-collins-mom-berates-sons-alabama-commitment-on-live-tv.

Hayes, Matt. "Alabama's Nico Johnson Carrying Heavy Burden into Title Game." *Sporting News.* 7 Jan. 2013. http://www.sportingnews.com/ncaa-football/story/2013-01-05/bcs-national-championship-alabama-vs-notre-dame-nico-johnson-uncle-died-mother.

Hays, Graham. "Alabama's Title a Milestone for SEC." *espnW.com.* 7 June 2012. http://espn.go.com/college-sports/softball/story/_/id/8017675/2012-womens-college-world-series-alabama-crimson-tide.

-----. "Alabama Wins at Speed of Sound." *espnW.com.* 25 May 2012. http://.espn.go.com/college-sports/softball/story/_/id/7970604/ncaa-softball-tournament-alabama-crimson-tide-wins-speed-sound.

-----. "Jackie Traina Lifts Tide to WCWS." *ESPN.com.* 28 May 2011. http://.espn.go.com/college-sports/blog/_/name/college_sports/id/6602578/traina-lifts-alabama-crimson-tide-wcws.

Hersch, Hank. "A New, Improved Tide." *SI.com.* 27 Sept. 1993. http://www.si.com/vault/1993/09/27/129358/a-new-improved-tide.

-----. "The Tide Rolls with a Shula Named Mike." *SI.com.* 27 Aug. 1986. http://www.si.com/vault/1986/09/08/113921/the-tide-rolls.

Hicks, Tommy. *Game of My Life: Alabama.* Champaign, Ill.: Sports Publishing L.L.C., 2006.

Higgins, Ron. "A Man of Crimson Cloth." *SEC Digital Network.* 4 Jan. 2013. http://www.secdigitalnetwork.com/SECNation/SECTraditions/tabid/1073/Article/240561.

-----. "Defense Lifts Alabama to 1993 National Championship." *Memphis Commercial Appeal.* Reprinted in *Sugar Bowl Classic: A History* by Marty Mule and found at allstatesugarbowl.org/site99.php.

-----. "Transfer Worked Wonders for Donnelly." *SEC Digital Network.* 30 Nov. 2012. http://www.secdigitalnetwork.com/SECNation/SECTraditions/tabid/1073/Article/

239842/transfer.

Hoffer, Richard. "Joe Namath the Qb and the Bear." *SI.com*. 17 Jan. 2013. http//www. si.com/vault/2013/01/17/106273078/joe-namath-the-qb-and-the-bear.

Holby, Pete. "Auburn vs. Alabama 2012 Final Score: Tide Dominates Every Part of Game in 49-0 Win." *SB Nation*. 24 Nov. 2012. http://www.sbnation.com/college-football/2012/11/24/3686780/alabama-auburn-2012-results.score.

Hyde, Dave. "Former Dolphin Tony Nathan Keeps His Promise, Graduates from College at 58." *South Florida Sun-Sentinel*. 7 May 2015. http://www.sun-sentinel.com/sports/miami-dolphins-tony-nathan-0508-20150507-column.html.

Inabinett, Mark. "Dwight Stephenson Mixes Christian Testimony, Bear Bryant Stories at FCA Event." *AL.com*. 20 March 2015. http://www.al.com/sports/index. ssf/2015/013/dwight_stephenson_mixes_christ.html.

Irvine, Steve. "Remembering Derrick Thomas." *ROLLTIDE.com*. 12 Sept. 2014. http://www.rolltide.com/sports/m-footbl/spec-rel/091214aaa.html.

Jones, Todd. "Tidal Wave." Yea *Alabama 2009*. Hanover, Mass.: Maple Street Press LLC, 2010. 4-16.

Jares, Joe. "Alabama Stole the Show." *SI.com*. 17 Oct. 1977. http://www.si.com/vault/1977/10/17/622751/alabama-stole-the-show.

Kausler, Don. Jr. "More Than Anything, Mal Moore's Love Story Stands Out." *AL.com*. 31 March 2013. http://www.al.com/sports/index.ssf/2013/03/more_than_anything_mal_moores.html.

-----. "Tide's Ben Eblen Emerging as the Backup Who Doesn't Back Down." *AL.com*. 2 Feb. 2011. http://www.al.com/sports/index.ssf/2011/02/tides_eblen_emerging_as_the_ba.html.

Kazek, Kelly. "The Original Mack Brown." *AL.com*. 26 Dec. 2013. http://www.al.com/living/index.ssf/2013/12/the_other_mack_brown_alabamas.html.

Kirk, Steve. "Tide Pride Showing in World Series Debut." *The Birmingham News*. 25 May 2000. 01-D.

Landry, Sean. "Alabama's Dana Duckworth Living the Dream as Head Coach." *Tuscaloosa News*. 16 April 2015. http://www.tuscaloosanews.com/article/20150416/NEWS/150419646?p=1&tc=pg.

Lawrence, Andrew. "The Strong and Very Silent Type." *SI.com*. 19 Jan. 2012. http://www.si.com/vault/2012/01/19/106151259/the-strong-and-very-silent-type.

Looney, Douglass S. "Unbeaten and Un-Tide." *SI.com*. 10 Oct. 1994. http://www.si.com/vault/1994/10/10/132193/unbeaten-and-un-tide.

Low, Chris. "Alabama's Seniors Share Unbreakable Bond." ESPN.com. 28 Nov. 2012. http://espn.go.com/blot/sec/post/_/id/56729/alabamas-share-unbreakable-bond.

-----. "Fate 'Smiles' on Tide's Hightower, Barron." *ESPN.com*. 5 Jan. 2012. http://espn.go.com/blog/sec/post/_/id/36322/fate-smiles-on-tides-hightower-barron.

-----. "Tide's Jones, Vlachos Always a Step Ahead." *ESPN.com*. 4 Nov. 2011. http://espn.go.com/blog/sec/post/_/id/32138/tides-jones-vlachos-always-a-step-ahead.

Maisel, Ivan. "Bama O-Line Bludgeons Notre Dame." *ESPN.com*. 8 Jan. 2013. http://.espn.go.com/college-football/bowl12/story/_/id/8803941.

-----. "Matchup Sparks Memories of Bear." *ESPN.com*. 10 Sept. 2010. http://www.sports.espn.go.com/espn/print?id=5551302.

-----. "Tide Proves They're a Perfect No. 1 in Flawed Contender Group." *ESPN.com*. 30 Nov. 2014. http://.espn.go.com/blog/sec/post/_/id/961604-tide-proves-theyre-a-perfect-no-1-in-a-season-with-no-dominant-team.

Mandel, Stewart. "Soft-Spoken Mosley the Key to Alabama's Vaunted Defense." *SI.com*. 6 Jan. 2013. http://www.sportsillustrated.cnn.

com/college-football/news/20130106/cj-mosley-alabama.

McNair, Kirk. "LSU Wins Defensive Struggle in OT." *Tide Rolls: Alabama's 2011 National Championship Season*. Chicago: Triumph Books LLC, 2012. 94, 96, 100.

Menzer, Joe. "Sweet Redemption." *NCAA.com*. 3 June 2013. http://www.ncaa.com/news/golf-men/article/2013-06-02/sweet-redemption.

Mitrosilis, Teddy. "Bama QB Beat UF While Honoring Auburn Student with Cancer." *FOX Sports*. 23 Sept. 2014. http://www.foxsports.com/college-football/story/alabama-qb-blake-sims-honors-auburn-student-cancer-florida-game-cfb-am-982314.

Montgomery, Kayla. "Alabama Volleyball Team Set to Succeed." *The Crimson White*. 7 Oct. 2014. http://www.cw.ua.edu/article/2014/10/alabama-volleyball-team-set-to-succeed.

-----. "Mainz Mania: UA Women's Tennis Coach Enters Nineteenth Season." *The Crimson White*. 17 Feb. 2015. http://www.cw.ua.edu/article/2015/02/mainz-mania-ua-womens-tennis-coach-enters-nineteenth-season.

Murphy, Austin. "Move Over, Gators." SI.com. 14 Dec. 2009. http://www.si.com/vault/2009/12/14/105886399/move-over-gators.

-----. "The End of the Run." *SI.com*. 11 Jan. 1993. http://www.si.com/vault/1993/01/11/127874/the-end-of-the-run.

"National Champion: Emma Talley Wins the NCAA Individual Crown." *RollTide.com*. 25 May 2015. http://www.rolltide.com/sports/w-golf/recaps/052515.aaa.html.

"National Champions: Women's Golf Wins First NCAA Championship." *RollTide.com*. 25 May 2012. http://www.rolltide.com/sports/w-golf/recaps/052512aa.html.

"Nico Johnson." *Wikipedia, the free encyclopedia*. http://en.wikipedia.org/wiki/Nico_Johnson.

"No. 1 Alabama Rides Cooper's 224 Yards, 3 TDs by Auburn." *SECsports.com*. 30 Nov. 2014. http://www.secsports.com/article/11951059/no-1-alabama-rides-cooper-224-yards-3-tds-auburn.

"No. 1 Alabama Silences Struggling Arkansas." *ESPN.com*. 20 Oct. 2013. http://www.scores.espn.go/com/ncf/recap?gameId=332920333.

Ostendrof, Greg. "Alabama QB Puts Iron Bowl Rivalry Aside to Honor Auburn Student with Cancer." *ESPN.com*. 22 Sept. 2014. http://www.espn.go.com/blog/sec/post/_/id/89172/sims-puts-iron-bowl-rivalry-aside-for-a-day.

Putnam, Pat. "Pride in the Red Jersey." *SI.com*. 11 Oct. 1971. http://www.si.com/vault/1971/10/11/612456/pride-in-the-red-jersey.

Reed, William F. "'Bama Roars Back." *SI.com*. 30 Oct. 1989. http://www.si.com/vault/1989/10/30/120900/bama-roars-back.

Scarborough, Alex. "A Different Kind of Win for Alabama." *ESPN.com*. 16 Sept. 2013. http://www.insider.espn.go.com/blog/colleges/alabama/post/_/id/16601/texas-am-a-different-kind-of-win-for-alabama.

-----. "Alabama Turns the Page to Mississippi State." *ESPN.com*. 11 Nov. 2014. http://www.espn.go.com/blog/sec/post/_/id/93290/alabama-turns-the-page.

-----. "Arkansas a Blast from Past for Alabama." *ESPN.com*. 15 Oct. 2013. http://www.espn.go.com/blog/colleges/alabama/post/_/id/17256/arkansas-offense-a-blast-from-the-past-for-alabama.

-----. "Collins Looking Forward to LSU Game." *ESPN.com*. 7 Nov. 2013. http://www.espn.go.com/college-football/story/_/id/9938530/alabama-crimson-tide-landon-collins-remembers-hateful-reaction-commitment.

-----. "Derrick Henry's Decision to Stay at Alabama Paying Dividends for All." *ESPN.go.com*. 16 Sept. 2015. http://espn.go.com/college-football/story/_/id/13668573/alabama-crimson-tide-star-derrick-henry-thought-transferring-freshman.

-----. "Kouandjio's Long Road to Alabama." *ESPN.com*. 29 Nov. 2013. http://www.espn.go.com/college-football/story/_/id?0051979/alabama-tackle-cyrus-kouandjio-took-long-route-cameroon-tuscaloosa.

-----. "Landon Collins Eager for the Next Chapter." *ESPN.com*. 25 Aug. 2014. http://espn.go.com/blog/sec/post/_/id/87143/colins-eager-for-the-next-chapter.

-----. "Reggie Ragland Finds Confidence, Emerges on Alabama's Defense." *ESPN.com*. 21 Oct. 2014. http://www.espn.go.com/blog/sec/post/_/id_91423/reggie-ragland-finds-confidence-emerges-on-alabamas-defense.

Scott, Richard. *Legends of Alabama Football*. Champaign, Ill.: Sports Publishing L.L.C., 2004.

"SEC Championship Game: #2 Alabama 32 — #1 Florida 13." Yea *Alabama 2009*. Hanover, Mass.: Maple Street Press, 2010. 64-69.

Simpson, Corky. "Blue Collar to Blue Chip." Yea *Alabama 2009*. Hanover, Mass.: Maple Street Press LLC, 2010. 81-82.

Staples, Andy. "Alabama Kicker Jeremy Shelley Enjoys BCS Championship Redemption." *SI.com*. 10 Jan. 2012. http://www.sportsillustrated.cnn.com/2012/writers/andy_staples/01/10.jeremy.shelley/index.html.

-----. "Alabama Recruit Grant Hill Shines at Rivals 100 Five-Star Challenge." *SI.com*. 25 June 2012. http://www.sportsillustrated.cnn.com/2012/writers/andy_staples/06/25/grant-hill-alabama-rivals-100/index.html.

-----. "Rolling with the Tide." *SI.com*. 17 Jan. 2013. http://www.si.com/vault/2013/01/17/06273076-rolling-with-the-tide.

-----. "The Perfectionist." *Sports Illustrated*. 20 April 2015. 75-77.

Terrell, Roy. "The Bear and Alabama Come Out on Top." *SI.com*. 11 Dec. 1961. http://www.si.com/vault/1961/12/11/621634/the-bear-and-alabama-come-out-on-top.

"Top 10 Alabama Crimson Tide Players of All Time." *Sporting News*. http://www.sportingnews.com/photos/4634843-top-10-alabama-crimson-tide-players-of-all-time/slide/299446.

Underwood, John. "Bama's Big, Bold Bid in the Week That Was." *SI.com*. 23 Nov. 1964. http://www.si.com/vault/1964/11/23/614109/bamas-big-bold-bid-in-the-week-that-was.

-----. "Sorry, But Alabama Had to Run." *SI.com*. 29 Oct. 1973. http://www.si.com/vault/1973/10/29/618410/sorry-but-alabama-had-to-run.

Wade, Don. *Always Alabama*: *A History of Crimson Tide Football*. New York City: Simon & Schuster, 2006.

Wertheim, L. Jon. "Underrated." *SI.com*. 25 Nov. 2013. http://www.si.com/vault/2013/11/25/106400019/underrated.

Wiley, Ralph. "How the Tide Has Turned." *SI.com*. 2 Feb. 1987. http://www.si.com/vault/1987/02/02/114791/how-the-tide-has-turned.

NAME INDEX
(LAST NAME, DEVOTION DAY NUMBER)

206

SCRIPTURES INDEX
(by DEVOTION DAY NUMBER)

208